BLOOD MOST PRECIOUS

EDWIN NEELY

BLOOD MOST PRECIOUS

Copyright © 2017 by Hayes Press

All rights reserved. Printed in the United Kingdom. No part of this book may be used or reproduced in any manner whatsoever without written permission except in the case of brief quotations embodied in critical articles or reviews.

Unless otherwise indicated, all Scripture quotations are from the Holy Bible, the New American Standard Bible®, (NASB®), Copyright © 1960, 1962, 1963, 1968, 1971, 1972, 1973, 1975, 1977, 1995 by The Lockman Foundation Used by permission. (www.Lockman.org). All rights reserved worldwide. Scriptures marked KJV are from the King James Version (1611, Public Domain).

Published by Hayes Press (**www.hayespress.org**)

The Barn, Flaxlands, Royal Wootton Bassett, Wiltshire, UK SN4 8DY

01793 850598

ISBN: 978-1-911433-29-3

First Edition: May 2017

10 9 8 7 6 5 4 3 2 1

CONTENTS

BLOOD MOST PRECIOUS i

CONTENTS 3

1: NON-SACRIFICIAL BLOOD 5

2: NON-ALTAR SACRIFICES 15

3: THE SANCTITY OF THE BLOOD 23

4: SPRINKLED BLOOD 29

5: THE BLOOD OF THE SIN OFFERINGS 37

6: THE BLOOD OF THE SWEET SAVOUR OFFERINGS 45

7: AN ALTAR DRENCHED WITH BLOOD 52

8: EFFECTS OF BLOOD FOR THE BELIEVER TODAY 59

9: THE CUP OF THE NEW COVENANT IN MY BLOOD 69

10: THE THREE CROSSES 77

11: OUR GREAT HIGH PRIEST 85

12: HALLELUJAH FOR THE BLOOD! 89

13: A SUMMARY OF KEY POINTS 95

REFERENCES 99

MORE TITLES FROM THE AUTHOR 102

MORE TITLES FROM HAYES PRESS 104

ABOUT HAYES PRESS 105

Bought with blood most precious,
Pardoned through His death,
Now a holy priesthood
(Thus the Scripture saith).
In Thy holy presence
We would humbly dwell;
Hearts by Christ redeemed
Songs of praises swell.
J. B. Belton

1: NON-SACRIFICIAL BLOOD

Some may feel quite squeamish or uneasy about a non-medical book concerned with blood, but may be more reassured when they learn that the Bible has no fewer than 375 verses (out of the 31,102 verses in it) that mention the subject. One would realise that with that kind of coverage the Holy Spirit is endeavouring to teach us something about its importance. Animal conservation activists will find repugnant the whole subject of animal sacrifice (as may most of us) and vegans and vegetarians may object to the consumption of some sacrificed animals that Israelites were commanded to eat; however, we are assured in Scripture that God does indeed love animals with a love even greater than those animal lovers possess.

The psalmist, David, said, "O LORD, You preserve man and beast.[1]" The law given through Moses specifically required that the Sabbath rest be extended to cattle.[2] The psalmist indicated that God would get praise from beasts and all cattle, from creeping things and winged fowl[3] - in fact, from everything that has breath[4]. The godly king Solomon wrote by the Spirit that a righteous man has regard for the life of his animal[5]. This is true; someone has said that even a pet dog will benefit from its master being a Christian believer. God Himself expressed His compassion for the great city Nineveh in Jonah's day, not only because of the citizenry there but because there were in it many animals[6]. Not even a sparrow falls to the ground without the concern of His Father, said the Lord Jesus. God cares for the animals He has created, but He cares for man whom He has created in His own image even more! "You are more valuable than many sparrows.[7]"

The writer to the Hebrews states: "… one may almost say, all things are cleansed with blood, and without shedding of blood there is no forgiveness.[8]" Man, the sinner, needs forgiveness. Animal sacrifice, a picture of the ultimate sacrifice of God's beloved Son, was a covering for the past until in the fullness of the time God sent forth His Son; that was God's answer to a world sunk in sin because of the wrong action of its first parents and because of the outworking of that sinful condition in each of our own human lives. It is the blood that makes atonement for the soul: "I have given it to you on the altar.[9]"

But not all blood mentioned in the Bible was the blood of altar sacrifice. Though not the first mention of blood in the Bible (the first was Abel's) one of the most touching Bible scenes describes aging Jacob[10], who had recently buried his beloved father, being shown the blood-stained tunic of many colours that he had given his son and coming to the conclusion that Joseph - his favourite, who had been sent on a mission by his dad - had in fact been torn in pieces and killed, possibly eaten by a wild beast.

We feel his agony at the thought, sorrow and mourning so intense that he felt he would die, unable to be consoled. And in the sorrow of men like Jacob, and later David who mourned so intensely for his son, Absalom, we get a faint picture of the heart of the Father who considered the shed blood of His only-begotten and well-beloved Son at Calvary. And the Spirit who inspired the writing of Scripture - Himself God, knowing the end from the beginning - caused prophets such as Amos to write of mourning for an only son as "a bitter day"[11], and Zechariah writing of the bitter weeping that accompanies the passing of a firstborn[12]. If considering Bible references to blood draws us closer to the heart of God, the exercise will be of great value indeed.

Not all blood in the Bible leads us to Calvary, however - not directly, anyway. Abel's blood crying to God from the ground[13], spilled by Cain the world's firstborn, gives us some idea of the import that God places upon it. Just what Cain knew about the subject of death we don't really know; certainly he hadn't seen much of it, if any. But he became a murderer in the hatred and jealousy of his heart. The life of the flesh is in the blood and the God who accounts life which He Himself creates to be very precious will have its misuse answered for, whether in sacrifice or in judgment. To Noah He said, "Surely I will require your lifeblood; from every beast I will require it. And from every man, from every man's brother I will require the life of man. 'Whoever sheds man's blood, by man his blood shall be shed, for in the image of God He made man.[14]'" He has not changed that statement.

Blood flowed in the past and will again in the future in unimaginable quantities - both times in judgment. When Moses was sent by God to bring the people of Israel out of captivity in Egypt, he was gifted with a series of plagues to bestow on Pharaoh and on his multitude of gods. No other society of its time possessed so many worshipped deities, and probably no other since Egypt has until today, when idols of all sorts abound - money and power being two of them. Many of the gods in Egypt's polytheism supposedly overlapped in their authority. Moses and the apostle Paul agree in their writings that idols are just a front for demons (see Deut.32:16,17 and 1 Cor.10:20), so Satan's activity at that time to frustrate the work of God in separating a people to Himself shows us something of the value that God places upon having that people, as Isaiah 43:21 testifies.

Khnum, alternately spelled Khnemu, was usually represented with a ram's head and was the guardian deity of the Nile's source; Hapi was worshipped as the spirit of the Nile; and Osiris, the god of the underworld and often referred to as simply "god" because of his importance - according to the Egyptians - had the Nile River as his bloodstream. Other lesser gods also had importance in the Nile's activity. The whole economy of that powerful land depended on the Nile for transportation, agriculture, religion; and the river was also its main water source for all bathing and human consumption. Moses told Pharaoh what would occur should he harden his heart against God in not releasing Egypt's Israelite slaves, and occur it did. Moses, at the command of the Lord, stretched his hand and rod over the river and tributaries, over pools, reservoirs and even containers of water in Egyptian homes. All became blood[15].

Was it literal blood or some chemical action in the water that made it appear so? Certainly, the power of God that later turned water to wine could turn water to blood. In any case, the fish died, the Nile became foul, and for a week the only water obtainable throughout the land was from shallow wells dug in desperation. Pharaoh's magicians, Jannes and Jambres, were able to produce similar results with little bits of water, further hardening Pharaoh's resolve. They might have been better employed turning the blood back into potable water had they really possessed magical powers. In any case Egypt, and Israel, who had embraced Egypt's worship, were clearly shown the superiority of the one true God over any demon-directed imaginations.

Unfortunately, Israel hung onto the demon-inspired idolatry that they picked up in Egypt and the whole evil persisted for generations even in their own land, a reason why, no doubt, they were also afflicted with the plague of blood. Ezekiel tells us that the whole position of the slavery of Israel in Egypt was because they had fallen in love with Egypt's gods[16]. Joshua had reported the same[17]. Not only did the river's foulness affect the local population, but the river of blood in divine judgment is also a foreshadowing (as are the other Egyptian plagues) of judgment yet to come in the days of the Tribulation, foretold in many prophecies of the Old Testament and so clearly in John's writings in the book of Revelation; this Tribulation will take place in God's judgment against the one and the many who raise a fist against the God of heaven.

When the bowls of the wrath of God at the end of the Great

Tribulation are poured out upon the earth years after those saved by the grace of God have been called to their reward, the nations remaining will be gathered to battle to the fertile valley of Armageddon in north central Israel. John the apostle then describes the scene: "And I saw heaven opened, and behold, a white horse, and He who sat on it is called Faithful and True, and in righteousness He judges and wages war ... He is clothed with a robe dipped in blood, and His name is called The Word of God.[18]"

That robe dipped in blood takes you back in thought to Joseph's blood-stained tunic, doesn't it? But this time the blood is the blood of Christ's enemies, for He has come in judgment to strike down the nations and to rule them with a rod of iron and He treads the wine press of the fierce wrath of God. Christ originally defeated His enemies by being trodden down in that same wine press, the blood which flowed being His own, but Isaiah sets the scene for us in prophecy: "Why is Your apparel red, and Your garments like the one who treads in the wine press? 'I have trodden the wine trough alone, and from the peoples there was no man with Me. I also trod them in My anger and trampled them in My wrath; and their lifeblood is sprinkled on My garments ... and I poured out their lifeblood on the earth.[19]'" John tells us: "And the wine press was trodden outside the city, and blood came out from the wine press, up to the horses' bridles, for a distance of two hundred miles.[20]"

Whatever the significance of the distances measured or the depth of the flow, the picture is one of the fierceness of the wrath of God, the destruction of the nations that oppose Him and His purposes and the utter physical hopelessness of any who withstand His will. One remembers the old Latin inscription in many a graveyard: *"Sic transit gloria mundi."* So passes the glory of the world. *"O quam cito!"* Oh, how quickly!

The river of blood from the divine wine press may well have been foreshadowed in the red river of the Nile back in Pharaoh's day. And the suggestion is amplified by the song that was sung shortly after its disclosure in Revelation: "And they sang the song of Moses, the bond-servant of God, and the song of the Lamb, saying, 'Great and marvelous are Your works, O Lord God, the Almighty; Righteous and true are Your ways, King of the nations! Who will not fear, O Lord, and glorify Your name? For You alone are holy; For ALL THE NATIONS WILL COME AND WORSHIP BEFORE YOU, FOR YOUR RIGHTEOUS ACTS HAVE BEEN REVEALED.[21]" A song of Moses and his people also rang out when Pharaoh's ambitions were eventually defeated; Moses' life of faithfulness and victory also ended in song once Israel had been brought to the border of the land of promise[22].

John's book of Revelation informs us further about blood and the judgments of God. John had been shown a book of judgment sealed with seven seals, each to be opened by the only One worthy to take the book and open the seals thereof, Christ Himself. At the opening of each seal John describes the outcome, and when the final seal is opened angels prepared to blow seven trumpets. At the sounding of the second trumpet, something that resembled a flaming mountain was thrown into the sea in his vision and a third of the sea became blood. Scientists estimate the amount of water in the seas to be about 321,000,000 cubic miles of water. Over 100,000,000 cubic miles, then, will be turned to blood; a third of the creatures in the sea will die; a third of the traffic sailing upon the sea will be destroyed. 71% of the earth's surface is covered with water. 96.5% of that water is in the oceans. The earth is to experience blood in judgment because it had shed the precious lifeblood of God's saints[23]. And this judgment at the blowing of the second trumpet is only the beginning of blood judgment.

Then John saw one of four living creatures in heaven which he had previously described give to seven angels seven bowls full of the wrath of God. When commanded, each of the angels in turn poured out God's wrath, and when the second angel poured his bowl into the sea it became blood like that of a dead man; and every living thing that was in the sea died[24].

One can readily observe the fulfilment of the words of Hebrews 1:10-11: "… THE FOUNDATION OF THE EARTH AND THE HEAVENS ARE THE WORKS OF YOUR HANDS; THEY WILL PERISH, BUT YOU REMAIN; AND THEY ALL WILL BECOME OLD LIKE A GARMENT, AND LIKE A MANTLE YOU WILL ROLL THEM UP; LIKE A GARMENT THEY WILL ALSO BE CHANGED." With climate change and the multiplication of natural disasters, we see that beginning to happen today. The whole of creation is heading towards what Peter prophesied in 2 Peter 3:10-11: "But the day of the Lord will come like a thief, in which the heavens will pass away with a roar and the elements will be destroyed with intense heat, and the earth and its works will be burned up." And Peter adds a word to us: "Since all these things are to be destroyed in this way, what sort of people ought you to be in holy conduct and godliness?"

The blood in the sea is described as that of a dead man. There was no life, no oxygen there. The blood of the dead cannot be used in transfusions, even today. It is good only for the drain. It was dead, putrefying blood; it was of the same character as the religion worshipped by both the Egyptians and the Israelites who had been corrupted by it in the past, and all those from all parts of the world arrayed in battle against the Lord in the future.

Following quickly after the second bowl was the pouring of the third, causing the rivers and springs of fresh water to become blood. "And," says John, "I heard the angel of the waters saying, 'Righteous are You, who are and who were, O Holy One, because You judged these things; for they poured out the blood of saints and prophets, and You have given them blood to drink. They deserve it.' And I heard the altar saying, "Yes, O Lord God, the Almighty, true and righteous are Your judgments.[25]"" The whole earth some time after the Rapture of God's own children will be awash with blood, for it poured out the blood of God's own Son and those who placed their faith in, and followed, Him.

The altar nowhere else in Scripture is recorded as speaking, though God at times spoke to Moses from between the cherubim on the ark of the covenant; but here the altar must speak - satisfied as the altar on which the Saviour died, satisfied that justice was finally secured. God's judgment is His own peculiar work[26], Isaiah tells us. The Hebrew writer says that "anyone who has set aside the Law of Moses dies without mercy on the testimony of two or three witnesses. How much severer punishment do you think he will deserve who has trampled under foot the Son of God, and has regarded as unclean the blood of the covenant by which he was sanctified, and has insulted the Spirit of grace?[27]"

These words were spoken to and about believing Christians whose salvation was secure. Peter adds to this: "… if [judgment] begins with us first, what will be the outcome for those who do not obey the gospel of God?[28]" The hymn writer explains the unbeliever's position:

> *"Sunk in ruin, sin and misery*
> *Bound by Satan's captive chains,*
> *Guided by his artful treachery*
> *Hurrying on to endless pain,*
> *My Redeemer plucked me as a brand from hell![29]"*

The rivers and seas of blood were punishment for having drunk the blood of prophets and saints, who were the people of God. Since punishment comes in differing intensities, what must be the punishment for all who crucified Christ? This chapter, describing some of the Biblical references to blood not used in sacrifice, ends in grief and judgment. Thankfully, the Christian believer need know nothing of that. There are brighter, if bloodier, chapters ahead describing and prescribing blessing unbounded to flow like rivers and oceans upon us who have accepted the truth of the shed blood of Christ on our behalf.

2: NON-ALTAR SACRIFICES

As a result of the LORD's directions from Mount Sinai and later, there were two broad categories of offerings - grain offerings (which, of course, did not involve the shedding of blood, though they were often offered in conjunction with blood offerings), and the slaying of animals which involved the disposition of the resulting blood. Disposition demanded certain defined instructions which, if not followed correctly, rendered the sacrifice ineffectual at least, or even brought death to the person responsible in some cases. Certainly, Numbers 18 promised death to the priest who mishandled something so sacred as the offerings to God.

There were sacrifices and offerings which had no place on the altar of God, however, and that omission was extremely important. Not all things offered speak to us about Christ's life and death. For instance, on occasion bread with leaven baked in it was to be offered - though it must never go to the altar - but in no way was leaven ever characteristic of the Saviour of whom most of the offerings spoke. The copper altar which stood in the court of the tabernacle, and later the permanent altar constructed under Solomon's direction which stood in the court of the temple in Jerusalem, was for sacrifices which pertained particularly to the people of God, not to the world at large.

The sacrifices not to be offered on the altar included the offering of the red heifer[1], the offering of another heifer for a dead body discovered in an open field[2], the Passover lamb and in most respects, the Sin offerings. These latter included guilt and Trespass offerings and were different from the former three in that the blood was, in fact, disposed of at the altar (and only portions of the animal's fat went on the altar) - and for most Sin offerings the carcass was consumed in a holocaust of fire somewhere clean, but outside the camp altogether.

When Moses waited on the mountain in the presence of God and to receive the tablets of the law, Aaron and Israel sinned below in the camp, going back to the idea of idol gods - graven calves that were supposed to have led them from Egypt. Some of Egypt's leading deities were shaped in the form of bulls or calves. It seems ironic that idol bulls were smashed by the command and action of Moses as things that had rendered the people unclean, but a heifer was taken to render them clean when by death they had become otherwise.

The reason for the slaying of the red heifer was itself unique. God is so holy that, though He was the One to deliver the sentence of death to all men, those who had turned to God became unclean through contact with the dead. God later told Ezekiel[3]: "'I have no pleasure in the death of anyone who dies,' declares the Lord God …", though there is a variation in that, for the psalmist writes: "Precious in the sight of the LORD is the death of His godly ones.[4]" God's holiness demands judgment for sin, but He takes no pleasure in that. This is evident in God's judgment of those who do take pleasure in judging when God uses men to carry out His strange work[5].

This matter of cleansing in relation to association with the dead was brought to a head when, because of disobedience, Israelites who had come out of Egypt as adults were told they would never enter the Land of Promise; their bodies would lie in the desert through which they passed until all of them had perished, save two faithful men – Caleb, the son of Jephunneh and Joshua, the son of Nun. Uncleanness was even brought upon anyone who touched a dead animal or swarming insect. Even the man who gathered up the ashes of the burnt heifer was unclean for the day. Special instruction was given with regard to a man put to death and hung on a tree; his body must not remain there overnight lest the whole land be defiled. As some have said, the one who hangs between heaven and earth is considered unworthy of either.

Be that as it may, the body that has surrendered life can bring uncleanness to others. God's purity demanded man's purity: "YOU SHALL BE HOLY, FOR I AM HOLY.[6]" This is true for us in this dispensation as it was for Israel under the Old Covenant. But God's grace provides man's remedy. It mattered not how a man came in touch with the dead, whether the touching of a grave or bone, the body of a stranger or close relative. It mattered not who, whether the most righteous Israelite or the stranger coming to sojourn amongst that people. All who touched the dead were defiled.

The red heifer, upon which had never come yoke and in which was found no defect whatever, was to be taken outside the camp, slaughtered and burnt to ashes in its entirety along with cedar wood, hyssop and scarlet wool, with the exception of a small sprinkling of blood toward the door of the tabernacle[7]. The ashes created were stored up and mixed with running water as required, to be used for the sprinkling on the person who had been defiled through contact with the dead. The water, not the ashes, was the thing sprinkled. It must be applied twice - once on the third day and again on the seventh.

The person in touch with the dead body would be unclean for a week. If the water were not to be sprinkled on the third day, the sprinkling of the seventh day would be ineffectual. While it is true that Israel over the centuries offered more than one red heifer (Hebrew sources record nine such offerings - the tenth, they say, to be offered by the Messiah when He comes), no second or future offering is specified in Scripture. Indeed, the Hebrews record specifies *the ashes of a heifer sprinkling those who are defiled*[8], not the ashes of heifers.

The picture offered is clear: Christ - spotless, undefiled - was offered outside the camp and the cleansing effect is perpetual. Sins yet to be committed are handled by His one offering. There will never again be a need for sacrifice for the sin or uncleanness of the world. Even in a future day Israel will know a fountain opened for sin and impurity - but it will be from the sacrifice of the Lord Jesus, to whom they will flee. We appreciate, however, that sweet savour offerings provided by the prince will again be offered in millennial Israel in praise to God. Expiation of sin or cleansing for uncleanness are not envisioned in that; devotion will be. The blood of the red heifer sprinkled with the finger towards the tabernacle shows the association with the purposes of God and the house of God with the sacrifice. The balance of the blood, along with the complete heifer including its refuse, was to be consumed in the fire.

There are three Hebrew words translated by the English word 'sprinkle'. The one used here indicates sprinkling with the finger dipped in blood, and is used in cases where blood is sprinkled before and on the mercy seat on the Day of Atonement or sprinkled before the veil in the holy place of the tabernacle. Another word, used in relation to sprinkling the blood on the altar, involves the use of a brush or some like implement to spatter droplets of blood on the object under consideration. Such a brush may well have been made of a cedar wood handle (probably rather juniper; cedar does not grow in the wilderness through which Israel travelled) and a hyssop sprig as a brush tip, tied on with scarlet string. This was used in applying the blood on the doorpost and lintel at the first Passover and may have been used in tabernacle service. Here, the whole thing was burnt with the sacrifice. By association with the blood, the brush became holy. All was totally consumed by fire, just as Christ was consumed by the fire of heaven: "He sent fire into my bones and it has prevailed over them[9]".

Another offering which was slaughtered outside the camp also involved a dead body. Numbers 35:33 clearly indicates that the illegal shedding of blood was extremely serious in the sight of God. It polluted the whole country in which the blood was shed and required the shedding of the blood of the murderer to atone for the land. It is worth serious contemplation that my sin might be the source of pollution to others. Perhaps this is what David had in mind when he prayed, "Let not those who hope in You be put to shame through me[10]."

There were times that would arise when the murderer could not be discovered. Lest the whole country be polluted by the killing a substitute must be provided, and Deuteronomy 21:1-9 explains just how that must be done. The settlement nearest the corpse which had been discovered in a field must provide a heifer which had never been yoked and bring it along with the local priests to a valley that had never been farmed or even ploughed and in which there was a running stream. Those who had brought the animal must decapitate the heifer (for that is what the sense is in the Hebrew language) and declare before the Lord their innocence in the matter of the corpse. It mattered not how far away that suitable valley might be or how busy the city elders or priests were - the shedding of blood was a serious matter and the purity of the whole country was at stake.

There was urgency to the needed cleansing. The atonement for the sin of the country would in no way absolve the murderer of his deed were he later to be discovered; but the shedding of blood demanded the shedding of blood - thus Calvary, if sinners were to be redeemed! Killers, either accidental or premeditated, could flee to one of the six cities of refuge in Israel until their cases might be decided legally, but unless blood was atoned for it continued to cry to God from the ground and polluted the whole land wherein it was spilled.

Perhaps the most notable blood that did not go to the altar mentioned in Scripture was the blood of the Passover lamb, shed on the night before Israel's departure from the iron smelting furnace of Egypt's slavery. The shedding of the blood of the paschal lamb was not sufficient in itself to save the threatened firstborn; the blood had to be applied as directed. The fact also that Christ's blood was shed for the sin and sins of the world is not sufficient to save today, either; there must be an application - the sinner must, on realising his condition, accept personally the shed blood as the propitiation for his sin.

The application of the collected Passover blood was with a brush of hyssop dabbed on the doorposts and latticed lookout window at the top of the door. Someone has suggested that it would be difficult to accomplish this without some blood being sprayed around and the resulting spray would form a cross upon the door, having the same effect as the mark or cross upon the forehead of certain righteous men as described by Ezekiel[11].

The same action would be performed for those who dwelt in tents in Egypt - for Israel, though enslaved, remained nomadic. Where the blood of the lamb was not applied, other blood was shed as the destroying angel went through the land taking the firstborn of man and beast. There was not a family among the Egyptians that was not affected. "When I see the blood I will pass over you"[12] remains a precious promise to those of us who have come to Christ for salvation.

3: THE SANCTITY OF THE BLOOD

We place a great deal of importance on things mentioned in Scripture for our learning - and matters which appear more than once in the Bible, especially so; for instance, the subject of baptism which comes up a dozen or so times. Surely the Holy Spirit is directing our thought towards something important! What import, then, must we place on a subject like blood which appears in 375 verses of the Bible?

The Hebrew word for blood is *dam*, which is linked to *Adam* and the word for earth, *adama*, from whence he was taken and (because of sin) to which he had to return. The word indicates "red" but according to later Bible verses it is blood and life that are inextricably united rather than blood and its colour. Though man after the great flood in Noah's day was permitted to eat animals, the blood, which was the life of the animal, was not ever to be eaten. Scripture repeats that over and over, and God curses lands and peoples which disobey that injunction. The prohibition of blood consumption began in Genesis 9:4, with Noah being warned. It continued through Leviticus and Deuteronomy as rigid law for Israel. Levitical law demanded death for disobedience of that command.

The matter is even one carried over into the New Testament, for though through His death the Lord Jesus cleansed many things previously unclean and changed some of the Old Covenant demands, the eating or drinking of blood was not one of them. The Jerusalem conference had revealed to it by the Spirit of God and through the conference that the people of God in Churches of God were to refrain from eating blood[1]. Blood has been eaten by some ethnic groups for many centuries, but the believer must refrain from black pudding (also known as blood pudding), duck blood soup, blood pancakes, blood sundaes, blood tofu and any other "delicacy" that contains blood. To God, the eating of blood is an abomination.

Also, blood was not to be associated with leaven in any of the offerings. Blood might go to the golden or the brazen altar as commanded, but though leaven was allowed - in fact commanded - in some offerings, they were not in any case to go to the altar. Blood-stained priests' garments must not be washed with the household laundry. It would be understood that in priestly activity accidents might invariably occur and priestly garb be stained, but priestly garments - holy in themselves and holy because of their contact with blood - must be washed in a holy place and the container in which the clothing was washed or boiled must afterwards be smashed if made of crockery or thoroughly scoured if metallic[2].

Furthermore, when Levitical offerings were being sacrificed, the importance of the blood is seen in the commanded order of the process: the blood must be disposed of first - whether its destination was to the veil, the altar or to the earth - before the remaining carcass was flayed, cut or offered on the altar. For the average Israelite, unwarranted approach to the tabernacle, which stood on holy ground because of the Holy One who dwelt between the cherubim on the mercy seat, would mean sudden death[3], just as approach to Mount Sinai would have done the same when God came down upon it. Numbers 18:32 makes clear that even for priest and Levite alike, mishandling of the ordinances of the Lord would result in death. Even the New Testament warns that it is a fearful thing to fall into the hands of the Living God[4]! The treatment of the blood was foremost in God's ordinances.

This matter, too, was carried over into New Testament worship, for the carnal Church of God in Corinth had explained to it how many among them were sickly and not a few were already dead[5] because of indifferent treatment of matters which God counted most serious - a strong imperative to those who handle the cup of the New Covenant in His blood in our day! Though that cup contains wine which never changes its character or becomes the blood of Christ as some believe, it speaks of the precious blood of Christ. In the Old Covenant, wine was poured out in drink offering on the ground. In the New Covenant, we are commanded all to drink of it[6]. We rejoice to do so, and should not just swallow it down as a ritual but consider that we are participating in the precious blessings afforded by the shedding of the blood of the Lord Jesus Christ.

Leviticus 17, a chapter dedicated almost totally to the subject of blood, is pivotal to a book which deals with cleanliness and order in the things of God. The first sixteen chapters delineate the sanctity of the whole sacrificial approach to God. The remaining ten chapters outline the necessity of the same dictates regarding the secular life of the people of God. In both sections, the value of sacrificial blood is prominent.

As we approach our God today, individually or collectively, or as we go about our secular lives as individuals or in fellowship with others, the blood of our great Sacrifice, the Lord Jesus Christ, is seen as most important. Hebrews 10:28,29 clearly shows the possibility of us falling away as far as our service for God is concerned: "Anyone who has set aside the Law of Moses dies without mercy on the testimony of two or three witnesses. How much severer punishment do you think he will deserve who has trampled under foot the Son of God, and has regarded as unclean the blood of the covenant by which he was sanctified, and has insulted the Spirit of grace?"

The lessons of Leviticus 17 can help us there. Israel had learned idolatry from the nations round about. In Egypt they became entrenched in it, so that even in release from captivity they persisted in carrying with them their idols and sacrificing in their open fields to goat demons. Peer pressure can have dire consequences. "Do not be deceived," says Scripture, "bad company corrupts good morals.7" Isaac Watts asked the question in one of his hymns: "Is this vile world a friend to grace to help us on to God?" It's a rhetorical question. You know the answer, and the lesson here is obvious. Jeremiah 13 shows a perfect example of the problem. He was told by the Lord to buy a waistband[8], so according to the command he did so, wore it close to his body, and then hid the thing in the earth.

After many days, told to get it again, he found it ruined - worthless because of where it had been. This vile world will do the same to us if we give it half a chance!

The Israelite must not sacrifice any of his animals at home, but bring his animal to the tent of meeting. There it would be humanely slain and the blood would be properly disposed of. There, God would get His portion, the priests theirs and the donor could rejoice in feasting upon the major portion of his gift knowing he had not been involved in demon worship and general evil, that God had been praised, and that the priest had received his portion. Any who refused to do that would be cut off from his people or even know the judgment of God directly against him in disease and death. Again God states: "For the life of the flesh is in the blood, and I have given it to you on the altar to make atonement for your souls; for it is the blood by reason of the life that makes atonement.[9]"

Wild game could also be eaten without bringing it to the altar, but its blood must be poured out on the ground and covered with earth. A man who ate meat killed by another animal, meat whose blood had not been properly drained and disposed of, brought uncleanness on himself. He must remain unclean until evening and must wash himself and his clothing; should he neglect this, he would remain unclean and bear the consequences. A priest must not eat of that animal whatsoever. Verse 4 of this seventeenth chapter of Leviticus uses the words "blood guiltiness" in connection with those who disobey its statutes. That's an expression used in relation to one guilty of murder, showing just how serious this matter of blood really is. With all this in mind, then, we can go on and examine in some detail just what is taught regarding the blood of the offerings and its relationship with the precious blood of God's great Offering, the Lord Jesus. Not stopping there, we will also examine some very practical applications of what we have learned.

4: SPRINKLED BLOOD

Much of the difficulty that we as Christian believers have in understanding Scripture is that we are unable sometimes to distinguish between the things that differ. Where God makes a difference, however, we had better learn to do the same; He intends that we should. Some have difficulty distinguishing between what belongs to the Old Covenant and what pertains to the New. Some have a problem seeing a difference between the Church which is the Body of Christ and what is termed in the Bible the Church of God or the house of God. Some are confused about what they see as falling away from salvation and falling from grace, or falling away in respect to Christian service. Some have difficulty distinguishing between which commandments pertain only to Israel and which pertain to believers under the New Covenant - and so on.

All of this tends to confusion, and because of this problem among people Satan has scored one of his greatest victories in causing disunity even among earnest Christian believers. God desires unity; Christianity today - while we may be one in Christ, brothers and sisters through our salvation - we are anything but so in matters of doctrine. There is only one truth, but man has sought out many inventions. God speaks through Hosea the prophet concerning Israel, but the same thing can apply today: "My people are destroyed for lack of knowledge.[1]" The apostle Paul exhorts Timothy and ourselves with these words: "Be diligent to present yourself approved to God as a workman who does not need to be ashamed, *accurately handling the word of truth*[2]" (emphasis mine).

To that point he also writes to the Church in Philippi: "And this I pray, that your love may abound still more and more in real knowledge and in all discernment, so that you may approve the things that are excellent [or that differ], in order to be sincere and blameless until the day of Christ.[3]" Paul was, by trade, a tentmaker. He knew practically what it was to cut a fabric incorrectly and then to hope to be able to sew it together correctly. One can imagine some funny-looking tents if that were done. As with fabric of tents, so with the fabric of Scripture; cut properly so that the results may be what were intended by the One who inspired it in the first place. He also says to the Roman church with the same intent: "... know His will and approve the things that are essential, being instructed out of the Law.[4]" All this is a lead-up to an understanding of the differences seen in the different types of the sprinkled blood of Scripture and differences in the teaching of the various offerings set out in the books of Exodus, Leviticus, Numbers, Deuteronomy and Ezekiel.

A practical word here may help would-be students of the Word. Martin Luther, whose study of the Scriptures revealed truths from them that shook the world - the western section of it particularly - said that he studied his Bible the way he gathered apples. First he shook the whole tree, that the ripest might fall; then he climbed the tree and shook each branch, every twig. Then he looked under every leaf. This is how we might also benefit more from our Bible study. Search the Bible as a whole. Read it as you would any other book. Then study it book after book noting the time sequence of each particularly; Bible books are not all arranged chronologically. Then give attention to the chapters, and after this carefully study the paragraphs and sentences. And you will be rewarded then if you search the meaning of the words. Sounds tedious? So is panning for gold or digging for diamonds, but oh, the rewards! I used to tell my students that it is what you learn after you know it all that will really set you apart. That is true in the things of God also.

Back in 1886, two French artists - Georges Seurat and Paul Signac - introduced an art form to the world later described as pointillism, in which small dots and dabs of colour rather than the smearing of paint by a brush or palette knife created the desired image. The system depended on the human eye to join the dots, producing the intended designs or portraits or landscapes. Bible study can be something like pointillism. Eventually, through the leading of the Holy Spirit, one's mind and spirit join the dots and we begin to see the whole picture. The Holy Spirit who inspired the word knew the end from the beginning; the Scripture is inspired with this knowledge. Though the various writers scarcely knew how their work would fit into the whole or even if it would, they contributed to that which is perfect and by the Spirit's help that which is in part is done away - we see the complete picture.

There are several Hebrew words translated 'sprinkle' in our Bibles. Among them two apply specifically to the handling of the blood of the offerings. 'Nazah' describes the dipping of the finger into the blood (or other substance) and shaking the blood in droplets upon the target.

'Zaraq' relates to the spattering of the liquid, say with a brush of hyssop, upon the desired object. This difference becomes important when we consider the action of the priests who sprinkled the blood and our understanding of the differences of application of the word in the New Testament. One thing we need to recognise is that to sprinkle the blood of a bullock with the finger on the altar would have taken an inordinate amount of the priest's day. As it was, to spatter it would keep him busy long enough.

To consecrate the priests Moses offered a ram for a burnt offering, sprinkling (zaraq) the blood on the altar. He then slew the second ram and placed blood on the right ear, right thumb and great toe of both Aaron and the priests' right foot, signifying the sanctification and dedication of what the priests heard, did and how and where they walked. Their garments were then sprinkled with blood and anointing oil, making them also holy. Previous to that, Exodus 24:6-8 depicts Moses taking the blood of peace and burnt offerings and applying it half to the altar and half upon the people. Hebrews 9:20,21 further enlightens us by saying that Moses sprinkled the book of the covenant, the tabernacle and all the vessels used in administering its services, all this on the basis of their profession of obedience to the commands of the Lord. The nation was now a covenanted people - both Israel, and those today who pledge obedience to follow those holy commandments.

This is what is referred to in the New Testament as the blood of sprinkling[5]. There remains today among a vast number of believing Christians bound for glory a small remnant who together seek to serve in covenant relationship as the people of God, described by writers of the New Testament as God's by the blood of sprinkling. We shall deal with the disposition of the blood of particular offerings in a separate chapter, for this matter is of prime importance to the thesis of this book.

It is important also to recognise that the sprinkling of the blood of the Passover, whereby the sign was placed on the doorposts and lintel of the Jewish dwellings in Egypt, is not what is referred to as the blood of sprinkling in such Scriptures as 1 Peter 1:2 or Hebrews 9:21ff, or Hebrews 12:24. The salvation of the children of Israel was an individual matter; they were not saved on that first Passover night as a nation, even though the whole nation was relieved of bondage. Those Israelites who had not applied the blood would have died with the Egyptians. Those Egyptians who did apply the blood would have been saved with the Israelites. We read in the Bible of the mixed multitude who came out of Egypt[6]. Such were some of them. Salvation was a private matter. What the nation did had little effect upon the responsibility of the individual.

But the blood of sprinkling applied months later by Moses the mediator of that covenant sealed it between a people - a nation attesting their obedience to the commandments of their God delivered through His servant Moses on Mount Sinai. It is not likely that Moses was able to sprinkle each of the millions who had come out to Sinai; so we individually belong to the Lord Jesus through cleansing by the blood of Christ, but God also sought out a people for Himself in our day, accomplished outside the nation of Israel but including any who believe, and this first occurred not at Sinai but on the day of Pentecost recorded in Acts chapter two. The blood of sprinkling is not depicted as the blood through which we were initially saved; it is now seen as the blood of a covenant based on obedience, and at the outset involving being saved, baptized and added, to and by the Lord (Acts 2:41,42).

Also, there are two types of cleansing: the cleansing from our sinful condition through faith in Jesus Christ and, secondly, the daily (or even better, hourly) cleansing from our sins just committed. The picture is painted on the night of Christ's betrayal. When Peter had a problem about having the Lord wash his feet he was told that in fact he had been washed totally, but there was a daily necessity of washing hands and feet literally[7], the same explaining the spiritual necessity for us all: we still do the things that we would not and leave undone the things that we should, and those matters must be dealt with in confession and repentance. Those who do not go to the length of daily washing of the hands and feet have no place in service for the Lord Jesus, saved through the initial washing though they may be.

The matter of the sprinkling of the water of cleansing from the ashes of the red heifer wherein was the burnt blood of the animal has already been covered; however, we must note that in the sprinkling of the water drained through those ashes the recipient became clean after the seventh day's cleansing, provided he had been also sprinkled on the third day of his uncleanness, but the one who administered the sprinkling became unclean through his handling of the matter. It is a serious lesson that I must learn, that my impurity affects the condition of others; others suffer because of my inadequacies.

The stumbling of others is a serious offence, as Scripture testifies. How careful I must be not to defile myself (and others) through my association with dead works, which I am to flee if I would serve the Living God.

This is demonstrated several times in any study of the Levitical offerings. The sprinkling on the third day doesn't seem to be required for any visible reason except that the Lord commanded it. The reason then seems to contain a lesson for us spiritually, for the things written beforehand were written for our learning as Paul tells the Romans in Romans 15:4, that through perseverance and encouragement of the Scriptures we might have hope - if you don't find cleansing in the day of opportunity there won't be cleansing when the days of opportunity are ended. Behold, now is the acceptable time; behold, now is the day of salvation! God is very gracious, often making up to us the days that the locust has eaten, but we must take advantage of the opportunities given for cleansing.

The Day of Atonement in Israel afforded further opportunity - indeed, requirement - for the priest to sprinkle blood. Both the blood of the bull that was offered for his personal atonement and the blood of the goat that was slain for the sins of the people were required to have a finger dipped in them quite separately and sprinkled before and on the mercy seat which sat on the ark of the covenant situated within the holiest of all[8]. This was that separate unit of the tabernacle - and, later, temple - which was available only to the high priest and only on that special day. Any other entrance of that compartment save to pack up the tabernacle for further movement of the whole people was punishable by death. What privilege the people of God have today to be able to be in the heavenly sanctuary itself week by week by the Spirit to present through our great High Priest praises acceptable to God concerning His Son and concerning Himself (see Hebrews 10:19-22; 1 Peter 2:5-9)! Well might I ensure that the water of cleansing has been fittingly applied. We find a parallel in Paul's first letter to the Corinthians, 11:28: "But a man must examine himself, and in so doing he is to eat of the bread and drink of the cup."

Blood, in conclusion, was placed on the book, the people, the furniture, the tabernacle, the ear, thumb and toe of the priests, the mercy seat, and before it, the horns of the golden altar, the horns of the copper altar, the walls of the copper altar, the base of that altar - all subsequent to the blood on the doorpost and lintel of the households of the nation and with different teaching associated with each application. This distinction takes the discernment pointed out at the beginning of this chapter. It comes with prayer and discipline of mind to the patient student of the word of God.

5: THE BLOOD OF THE SIN OFFERINGS

Within the broad category of blood offerings there were divisions: the Burnt offering, where the whole animal was sacrificed on the altar to the LORD with the exception of the skin which was the priest's, his reward for the work of offering the carcass and blood; the Peace offering, which was only partially for the altar, partly for the priest and the bulk to be eaten by the offerer and his family, a sweet picture of fellowship in that which is sacrificed; the Sin offering, which did not go to the altar, save the fat and kidneys and gall bladder; and within the Sin offering division there were also variations: the Sin offering, the Guilt offering and the Trespass offering, each of these for different categories of sins.

One major discernible difference between Burnt and Peace offerings and Sin offerings was that God smelled a sweet savour from the burning of the former, but not the latter. Burnt offerings went to the copper altar for consumption, small parts of the Peace offering likewise, and there were small parts of the Sin offerings that likewise were burnt on the copper altar; but those altar parts of the offerings for sin - the kidneys and gall bladder and fat - are never mentioned in connection with any sweet savour or aroma. All those that were in the sweet savour category burned gently all the day and all the night on which they were presented. It was the priests' duty to see that the fire never went out. It had been lit by God; it must not be extinguished, even being carried in fire pans while travelling.

The main parts of the Sin offering were consumed outside the camp in a holocaust of fire and brought God no sweet-smelling aroma. We can imagine the difference between the Burnt offering and Sin offering by thinking of the aroma of a roast of beef roasting gently in the oven and the same roast burning to smokey ashes. The blood of these different offerings was handled differently, each with different lessons for us. These paragraphs describe the Sin offering blood, and even that had variations to it depending on just whose sin necessitated the sacrifice. The early chapters of Leviticus need to be read carefully for us to ascertain the differences, but this reading is worthwhile for the things that differ here will bear on things that differ for us as we apply the teaching to the blood of our great Sacrifice, the Lord Jesus Himself, and to our understanding of the cup of the New Covenant in His blood of which we partake week by week in His grace. All this has an effect upon just how we frame our giving of thanks, for our entrance into the holies is to be with oral boldness - the Greek meaning of the word.

In the case of Sin offerings for the individual Israelite, the size and therefore the quality of the offering depended upon the state of responsibility among the people possessed by the sinner. If a priest, or even the high priest, sinned he must offer a bull - and that the finest in his herd. As time went on, Israel failed in this until Malachi writes: "'But when you present the blind for sacrifice, is it not evil? And when you present the lame and the sick, is it not evil? … But cursed be the swindler who has a male in his flock and vows it, but sacrifices a blemished animal to the Lord, for I am a great King,' says the Lord of hosts, 'and My name is feared among the nations.'[1]" God, who never would be anyone's debtor, would recompense the cheerful giver with even more and better than he had had before.

The handling of the blood was also commensurate with the state of the sinner. The matter is shown in the difference between Zechariah and Mary, both of whom questioned the angel about the unusual birth of a new child. Zechariah, the priest, was made mute for a season as a reprimand for disbelief, while Mary went without censure even though she questioned the whole operation. In the priest's case of sin, some of the blood must be brought into the holy place of the tabernacle and sprinkled with the finger seven times before the veil that separated the holy place from the most holy. The priest's service was directly to and on behalf of God in that holy place. God would be satisfied with the sprinkling of the blood there.

Then a little bit of blood was put on the horns of the golden altar, the altar on which incense was offered daily, which stood within the holy place and pertained to the most holy place beyond the veil. Through sin the priests' service at that altar was affected and the matter must be adjusted by the application of blood. The balance of the blood of the bull of the Sin offering must then be poured out at the base of the altar which stood outside in the court of the tabernacle, the copper altar. All aspects of the priestly work were rendered ineffective by sin until this atonement was made in the application of the blood. The whole operation, done with all due decorum and priestly dignity, would take no longer than fifteen minutes - mark that time - though the subsequent washing and cutting of the altar pieces and the taking of the bulk of the bullock out to a clean burning site might take just a little longer.

If the whole congregation were to sin, the activity with the blood would be identical to the offering for the priest. Again, every avenue of service was ineffective until the particular sin was cancelled by the blood of atonement. We often see in Scripture Israel sinning as a nation. In our day, we confess our own personal sins and God forgives according to His grace. We possibly seldom confess our sins committed by a Church or as a people for God. The leaders of God's people today certainly need sustaining prayer, for it would be through their misdirection, most likely, that the whole people might be caused to sin. Special earnest prayer should ascend when the worldwide conference of elders meets lest it lead to the whole people committing sin; the example for that meeting is the Jerusalem conference of Acts 15:1-29.

Daniel, the prophet, gives us an excellent example in this matter, for he is found on his knees confessing not only his own problems but the sins of his people[2]. Israel certainly sinned as a people at Shittim due to the temptation suggested by Balaam to Balak, King of Moab[3]. As a result, the judgment of God descended: Moses was instructed to kill the leaders of the people and 24,000 died that day. The number would have been greater had not Phineas, the priest, displayed his zeal for the LORD. Israel was later told to remember from Shittim to Gilgal[4] that they might know all the righteous acts of the LORD. The sin, the one whose zeal stopped the judgment, the passing of the flood of the Jordan on dry land, the cairns of remembrance and the eventual rolling away of the reproach of Egypt from the people, all parallel our own condition from sin to redemption, but the occurrence demonstrates the corporate sin of the nation and the judgment that might fall should intentional sin have its way.

The Churches in the New Testament referred to in Revelation 2 and 3 certainly sinned as Churches, with even the threatened removal of lampstands should problems not be rectified. Like Solomon, those who would lead God's people have a great need for wisdom! The seven Churches in Asia in the time of John the apostle were certainly marked out in that regard. Perhaps in our confession of sins to the Lord (see 1 John 1:9) we might keep this collective consideration in mind for both confession and supporting prayer?

If a leader sinned unintentionally (and incidentally, all these offerings were for unintentional sin; intentional sin was handled in judgment, but that is largely separate from our study here) the blood of his goat - a lesser offering than the bull - was to be put on the horns of the copper altar and the balance was to be poured out at the base of the altar; again, a very quickly-accomplished task, though done with all due respect and dignity. An individual without specific portfolio would bring a female goat or lamb and the blood would be handled in precisely the same way; again, a relatively short period of time as far as it concerned the priest who functioned at the altar on behalf of the person who needed atonement for his unintentional misdemeanour.

A Guilt offering was a variation of the Sin offering in that it dealt with a variety of specific sins such as neglecting to testify when requested, or touching something unclean unintentionally, or swearing thoughtlessly to do something and then not fulfilling the rash promise. Leviticus 7:7 tells us that the Guilt offering was like the Sin offering and the one law applied to both. When the sin involved loss to the LORD in the matter of holy things or to another person in any way, the Trespass offering aspect of the Sin offering demanded abundant repayment. But it is the blood of those offerings that we are particularly concerned with.

A person whose guilt must be dealt with would give according to his ability, not his station, a female lamb or goat, a couple of doves or young pigeons or a tenth part of an ephah of fine flour. The offering of a grain offering here no doubt partially explains the Hebrews writing that it almost might be said that all things are cleansed by blood[5]. Some things were also cleansed with fire, others with water, but all according to divine command, not men's wish. The Trespass offering was provided to assist the accused person who must make restitution and had more severe requirements about his offering, but the handling of blood was the same - spattered on the side of the copper altar; and in the case of the birds, some of their blood spattered and the balance poured out at the altar base - a fairly short job at best, considering that the lamb or goat or ram of the Guilt offering would possess less blood by far than the bull of the Burnt offering.

Further study of other aspects of the Levitical offerings will repay the student many times over in his or her contemplation of the fulfilment of these great types seen fulfilled in our Lord Jesus. Our concern here is the fact that most, if not all, of a priest's time was spent in handling the sacred things of the altar, and among these the time spent on the Sin offerings was minimal compared with the number of hours spent on the service of the sweet savour offerings - the Burnt offering and the Peace offering - particularly in the disposition of the blood.

6: THE BLOOD OF THE SWEET SAVOUR OFFERINGS

As has been said, the priests' working day involved a majority of their time serving at the altar and, since the Sin offering had only a minimal number of parts burned there, most of the time was spent in distributing the blood of the sweet savour offerings according to God's commandment. While the Sin offering took little time comparatively, the sweet savour offerings took considerably more. Read again Leviticus 1:5,11; Leviticus 3:8-13.

No matter what animal was sacrificed for the Burnt offering, or whether it was from the herd or the flock for a Peace offering, the blood must be collected and then spattered upon the sides of the copper altar, probably with the brush of hyssop mentioned previously. To so distribute the blood as though roughly painting it on would consume much more time than simply pouring the bulk of the blood out on the ground as with Sin offerings.

Indeed, the handling of the detail of the spreading of the blood (the washing and cutting were the job of the offerer) and the arranging on the altar of the wood and the altar pieces and correctly burning the whole Burnt offering and likewise painting or splashing on the blood of peace offerings (since all meat from domestic animals must be processed as Peace offerings) would have taken up most of the priests' daily ritual. They would go home tired at night. And though David arranged for teams of priests to serve while others rested, there was good reason to begin serving only after reaching maturity at 25 and retiring at age 50 as commanded through Moses by God. After the age of fifty, priests might volunteer to assist here and there and especially, I suppose, on festal occasions when the number of offerings was multiplied - but a daily workload was forbidden by God.

Of course, while some of the offerings had their beginning at Sinai, Burnt offerings did not originate with Moses and the people of Israel - though some of the rules concerning them would have been given only then. After the flood, Noah offered Burnt offerings of all the clean animals taken from the ark, and God smelled the sweet savour. Abraham offered the ram caught in the thicket by its horns as a Burnt offering in place of his son Isaac, who also was to have been offered as a

Burnt offering. From the offering of Noah we learn that God delighted in the sweet savour He smelled, and since He delights to pour blessings upon those with whom He is well pleased the whole of humanity knows His abundant goodness through blessings offered at that time to Noah, which we remember gladly every time we see a rainbow.

From Abraham's offering we learn that God accepted animal sacrifice - the shedding of its blood - in the place of the death of a human being; also that the whole picture of resurrection is to be associated with the Burnt offering for, as the New Testament says, in a figure Abraham received his son as resurrected from the dead[1], and indeed (had he been a Burnt offering) from the very ashes themselves. This resurrection aspect is a truth that affects us even today as we remember weekly the death of the Lord Jesus and what followed. God's commendation of Abraham's willingness to sacrifice that which was so precious to him shows His great pleasure in what was anticipated on Moriah's mountain.

Moses and Aaron informed Pharaoh that Israel must be freed to go into the desert and offer Burnt offerings. Burnt offerings were not for atonement for sin. They were often commanded as being offered in conjunction with Sin offerings, but they themselves were to demonstrate the total dedication either of the nation or the individual who offered; they were not for sin, but for devotion. Ephesians 5:1,2 may help us here: "Therefore be imitators of God, as beloved children; and walk in love, just as Christ also loved you and gave Himself up for us, an offering and a sacrifice to God as a fragrant aroma." Christ was the fulfilment of the Sin offering, certainly, but He also offered Himself to God as a whole Burnt offering, a sacrifice of devotion well pleasing to His Father.

We offer our Burnt offerings in praise to God, but that is acceptable on the basis of our offering of total self as described in Romans 12:1,2: "Therefore I urge you, brethren, by the mercies of God, to present your bodies a living and holy sacrifice, acceptable to God, which is your spiritual service of worship." Jeremiah's message to Israel included warnings to us as well: God will not be petitioned or accept the praises of those who give no heed to His commandments[2].

The psalmist in Psalm 100:3 reminds us that "We are His people and the sheep of His pasture." That pasture was the source of sheep for dedication to the Lord in sacrifice. Paul picks up the thought in Romans 8:36: "FOR YOUR SAKE WE ARE BEING PUT TO DEATH ALL DAY LONG; WE ARE CONSIDERED AS SHEEP TO BE SLAUGHTERED." We may never experience that physically, though in this world one never knows. But we are in the position spiritually of being crucified to the world and the world to us, given fully to God, giving fully to God. All the offerings were "slain before the Lord." And we, whether we live or whether we die, we also do it unto the Lord[3]. But when we offer our thanks it is not to the people there with us, though they might be edified by it; it is to God we are speaking. He knows the thoughts of the heart. It is good to remember that fact.

The Lord Jesus told the story of the unrighteous steward, one who squandered his master's goods and consequently lost his job[4]. Too old to labour physically and too proud to beg, he concocted a plan to endear himself to others at the expense of the man who had terminated his employment. He went to his former master's debtors asking them how much they owed to him and settled with them for a percentage of the true debt. In exactly the same way we have an adversary who whispers to us that we can get by, by giving 50% or 80% of what we owe. But what do you owe my Master? Consider in your answer the shedding of His blood for you and consider its application. The hymn writer wrote:

What shall I give Thee, Master? Thou who didst die for me ...
   Shall I give less of what I possess, or shall I give all to Thee?
What shall I give Thee, Master? Thou hast redeemed my soul.
   My gift is small, but it is my all, surrendered to Thy control.
What shall I give Thee, Master? Thou hast giv'n all for me.
   Not just a part, or half of my heart. I will give all to Thee!
     What shall I give Thee, Master, Giver of gifts divine.
I will not hold time, talent or gold. For everything shall be
                 Thine! [5]

That should be our aim as well.

Burnt offering blood might be spread before the Lord on the copper altar on behalf of the people who were for Him, or for individuals who out of the fullness of their hearts brought from their best to their God. Burnt offerings were commanded to be offered on behalf of the nation twice daily; on the Sabbath they were doubled; they were to be offered on the first of the month, again on festal occasions such as Leviticus 23 outlines: the Passover, Feast of Unleavened Bread, Waving of the Wave sheaf, Feast of Weeks, Feast of Trumpets, Day of Atonement.

As well, Burnt offerings were commanded to accompany Sin offerings for cleansing of a woman after childbirth, for cleansing of a leper or of a man or woman with a discharge, for the cleansing of a Nazirite who had become defiled, as well as for the consecration of the priests. This list will help us understand just how busy the priests were with the blood on the altar. It is said that a volunteer is worth a thousand conscripts. It may well have been that the voluntary offering from a full heart brought even a sweeter aroma to the God of heaven than the commanded ritualistic demands of Israelite daily activity. The appreciative heart, touched by the blessings of God, might bring his thankfulness in this way very often.

One noticeable feature of the Burnt offering by the individual was the interaction between the offerer and the priest. The offerer was very much involved in the whole process (except for the offering of the birds, the lesser offering); he must firstly choose and bring the offering, lay (or rather, press) his hand on its head identifying himself with it, slay it, and after the blood had been collected and distributed by the priest the offerer must skin the sacrifice and cut it into its various pieces ready for the altar. The priest served at the altar arranging both the wood and the sacrifice for burning, but the offerer must wash the legs and entrails for the further offering by the priest.

This interaction is a sweet picture of exactly what occurs as we bring our sacrifice of praises to the God and Father of the Lord Jesus Christ. There is a beautiful interaction of the Spirit-led offerer who speaks on behalf of the people and the great High Priest who perfects our feeble praises and presents them to His God and Father, for our access to the Father is through the Son. The Peace offering also displayed the fellowship between priest and offerer, each feasting on the animal slain; each assuring that God also got His full altar portion.

Of our High Priest, before He was such, it is written that He was daily God's delight but His delight was with the sons of men. It was not that He preferred men over His love for God, but there was a sweet harmony among the three due to His work. The Peace offering aspect of our service in the holies sends us home both edified and encouraged as we have feasted on the sacrifice of Christ. We often sing, "And all assembled cause to feel the presence of our God.[6]" As we feel His presence our souls are thrilled and filled.

The priests giving so much more of their time to the Sweet Savour offerings than to the Sin offerings might give us some thought about how much of our worship should be divided accordingly. We must be thankful, granted. But we must not overlook God's delight in having us appreciate Him and the Lord Jesus for who and what they are, rather than for their works' sake alone. John 14:11 gives us a clue in this regard: "Believe Me that I am in the Father and the Father is in Me; otherwise believe because of the works themselves." Appreciating the works of Christ seemed to be inferior to accepting Him for who He Himself really is.

7: AN ALTAR DRENCHED WITH BLOOD

The altar which stood in the court of the tabernacle in the wilderness and later in the land until the time of Solomon was relatively small, about seven and one half feet square and four and one half feet high, made of acacia wood and overlaid with bronze protecting the wood from the fire within which probably burnt on a base of earth. Many years later when Israel was settled in the Land of Promise, Solomon, given the task to erect a permanent home for the altar, constructed an altar thirty feet square and fifteen feet high.

Presumably there had to be a ramp leading up to it and a ledge for the priests to work and walk on. We are not told the dimensions of the altar in the post-exilic temple, but presume the size to be similar to the Solomonic altar. In any case, it is probably this latter structure that Zechariah was referring to in chapter 9 and verse 15 of his book as an example of absolute fullness - a sacrificial basin (the kind that would contain the blood of a bullock) and a picture of something absolutely inundated - the altar drenched with blood, particularly at the corners. According to Moses' instructions all containers associated with the altar were made of brass. A brass basin or bucket full of the blood of a bull would weigh about seventy pounds. A priest would have to be in good physical health to accomplish his work, no doubt a practical reason why those born into a priestly family who had a physical defect were not able to serve. There are spiritual lessons here for us also. For us, spiritual deficiencies comparable to the priests' physical deformities will hinder us from full participation in the service of God though we may, by God's grace, partake of the benefits.

The Burnt offering very often consisted of a bull, and the amount of blood in a full-grown bull is 20 litres, about 5 American gallons or 4 Imperial gallons. The amount of blood drained from a full-grown sheep or goat is much the same as contained in a human, about 6 litres. The daily supply of Burnt offering blood commanded would be dwarfed by the amount required on a festal day. For instance, the blood from Burnt offerings on the first day of the Feast of Tabernacles, the fifteenth day of the seventh month, would be taken from 13 bulls, 2 rams and 14 lambs. That's about 65 gallons. Add to that the daily demand, plus any voluntary offerings of people celebrating the event (for the command of God was that the people during that feast would be altogether joyful) plus the blood of any Peace offerings brought as people travelled from far and near to be at one of the three compulsory gatherings on Mount Zion.

David is reported to have offered on one occasion 1,000 bulls, 1,000 rams and 1,000 lambs all for a Burnt offering. That's 20,000 litres from bulls alone, 4,000 imperial gallons, plus nearly another 2,000 gallons from the rams and lambs. At the dedication of the temple in Jerusalem, Solomon offered a Burnt offering of 22,000 bulls and 120,000 sheep, all according to the Law of Moses. That is a total of 1,044,000 litres of blood to be spread in droplets on the four fifteen by thirty foot walls of the copper altar—an altar drenched by blood, indeed - and not for sin, but for a sweet savour, a devotion to the majestic God of heaven.

Historians of the time reported that the blood of a bull covered the walls of the altar twice, that is two complete paint jobs by a priest handling just one bull's blood. The priests were certainly busy that dedication day! Where did that amount of blood end up? Those who visit the Dome of the Rock in Jerusalem have an opportunity to examine the threshing floor of Arauna on which the altar stood from the cave beneath. Looking up to the cave's ceiling will reveal two holes, possibly there originally to assist in storage of grain in the cave beneath after threshing, but in the days of the temple directing the blood poured out down towards the wadi of the Kidron. That latter day described was one where the river ran with blood. Indeed, it probably ran more with blood for the altar than water from its source.

The point of all this is to underline that the matter of the work of the priests in Israel was more largely given to devotion - to the praises of God's people for who and what God is - rather than the consideration of the forgiveness of sin and sins, important and thanks-producing as that may be.

While most of the time was taken up with sweet savour offerings, the service of the priests on the altar was very sensitive to sin. When Israel sinned, the altar on whose service they depended became unclean to them, unable to fulfil its purpose on their behalf. Because of this, blood of the Sin offering must be applied to the horns of the altar. In the same way, heaven is tainted by the association of an earthly people even though they have been called with a heavenly calling. Heaven must have the blood of a Sin offering applied that the way might be opened for us in the Spirit and, of course, in our future entrance to it.

Christ supplied that need, not with the application of physical blood but in type. Someone has written: "The thought of atonement for the altar particularly after the anointing referred to in earlier verses seems strange, and it is not until we investigate the (Hebrew) word "chat" which has been translated "purified" that we realise how much has been lost in the translation. This word means 'to miss the mark' and from it comes the word for trespass. Hence the thoughts associated with the putting of blood on the horns of the altar are really concerned with a trespass against the altar, whereby it becomes defiled. In all of these cases of individual sin the offerer was caused to understand that when the blood was put upon the horns of the altar it showed that there had been a missing of the mark. His sin was an offence against the altar of burnt offering and without that altar being sanctified and without atonement for it being made it was unable to fulfil its purpose in connection with sweet savour offerings. He was caused to realise that his sin affected the altar, and while it remained unforgiven there was an effect upon the reception by God of that which was His due. The sinner may never have realised this, but when the blood was put upon the horns of the altar he realised it was unclean until it was sanctified by the pouring out of the blood of the sin offering at the base of the altar. Then atonement was made.[1]"

It is important to remind ourselves again that there is a difference between Christ's dying for sin and His dying for sins, both of which He accomplished at Calvary. John the Baptist's revelation in John 1:29 was concerning "the Lamb of God who takes away the sin of the world." Hebrews 9:26 states the same: "But once at the end of the ages He has been manifested to put away sin by the sacrifice of Himself." This aspect deals with the sin condition brought about by the first man, Adam as Romans 5:12 says: "Through one man, sin entered into the world, and death through sin …" That matter had to be set straight before our sinful actions could ever be atoned for.

Then we have 1 Corinthians 15:3: "Christ died for our sins according to the Scriptures" and similar verses, such as 1 John 1:9: "If we confess our sins, He is faithful and righteous to forgive us our sins and to cleanse us from all unrighteousness," which point out a secondary effect of Christ's death. Other verses include 1 Peter 2:24: "He Himself bore our sins in His body on the cross …" And Hebrews 9:28: "Christ also, having been offered once to bear the sins of many, will appear a second time for salvation without reference to sin, to those who eagerly await Him." Without the forgiveness of sin there could never have been the forgiveness of sins. Our thanks to God is for both. But we move on then from thanks in our Remembrance and an appreciation and proclamation of the Lord's death to praise for His resurrection and all that He and the Father and Spirit are - their characteristics, their majesty, their sweetness. Oh, the wonderful power in the blood of the Lord Jesus! How precious that God has given us so much that points forward to that shedding and cleansing, things that we might meditate upon in His presence!

8: EFFECTS OF BLOOD FOR THE BELIEVER TODAY

While meditation on the multitude of Old Testament writings pointing forward to Christ will prove rewarding, there are some very pertinent facts that take us beyond the cross as it applies to our salvation and present truths that should affect our lives as believers today. Careful consideration of the following Scriptures will provide grist for our meditational mills, things which we may not have thought about in depth previously. In the teaching profession, we were taught that there is no teaching unless there is learning by those taught; learning can be measured by changes in behaviour. Unless the verses change our behaviour or convince our minds that we are doing the right things already, there is not much evidence of teaching in these words of truth.

In Acts 20:28 the beloved Luke records Paul's final words to the leaders of the Church in Ephesus when he bids a final farewell to them as he prepares to leave forever the shores of that area. Those elders may have had to travel many miles to get to Paul - some scholars say as many as 40, though some say no more than 10 - but in its day even 10 miles made a journey. Paul tells them: "Be on guard for yourselves and for all the flock, among which the Holy Spirit has made you overseers, to shepherd the church of God which He purchased with His own blood."

We see immediately why readers have had difficulty with these words. Does God have blood? "God is Spirit[1]," and "A spirit does not have flesh and bones as you see that I have[2]." And then we realise that translators from the Greek have put in English words that do not give a true sense of the original. That verse might better have been translated, "… which He purchased with the blood of His own." It was the blood of God's own Son by which He purchased sinners, individual by individual. But this is more than that. He can't be referring to the Church which is the body of Christ - overseers have no responsibility there. Here it is the Church of God which He also purchased and that, I take it, is not the Church in Ephesus whose overseers were present on the beach but the whole Church as mentioned in 1 Timothy 3:15, which says: "I write so that you will know how one ought to conduct himself in the household of God, which is church of the living God, the pillar and support of the truth." That being the case, overseers are not just responsible for their own Assembly, but are overseers in the complete household of the faith. One wise writer has written: "The house of God and the body of Christ should never be confused and confounded; such distinctions as men and women (i.e. males and females), overseers and deacons, are not in the latter as they are in the former. There are many other distinctions in these widely different things.[3]"

As well as the personal salvation of you and me through the blood of Christ, then, He has purchased a prize for God which is open for believers to be a part of, described by Peter in this way: "But you are A CHOSEN RACE, A ROYAL PRIESTHOOD, A HOLY NATION, A PEOPLE FOR GOD'S OWN POSSESSION, so that you may proclaim the excellencies of Him who has called you out of darkness into His marvelous light; for you were once NOT A PEOPLE, but now you are THE PEOPLE OF GOD.[4]" Besides our salvation, then, we can rejoice in being part of a blood-bought, peculiar (in the sense of unique) people to delight the Father of the Purchaser. We can enjoy this delight in a very special way as with holy boldness we approach God's throne Lord's Day by Lord's Day to remember His Son and to praise His name. We can rejoice as we do as early Churches did, continuing steadfastly in the apostles' teaching, the fellowship, the breaking of the bread and the prayers[5].

Scripture states concerning Christ and His blood yet another fact: "… not through the blood of goats and calves, but through His own blood, He entered the holy place once for all, having obtained eternal redemption[6]." Of old, the High Priest entered the holy place in the earthly sanctuary year by year on the one

Day of Atonement, the tenth day of the seventh month of each year. Christ as our great High Priest entered the holy place in heaven though His own blood, not through the sacrifice of animals; but He has entered as High Priest which He was named in resurrection, a High Priest forever after the order of Melchizedek. Having obtained eternal redemption through His Calvary experience, He now lives forever as sympathetic priest to administer the benefits of that redemption to a priestly people, as Peter outlines in 1 Peter 2:10. Christ did not enter *with* His own blood, but by means of it. By God's grace we also have that holy privilege: "Therefore, brethren, since we have confidence to enter the holy place by the blood of Jesus" (Hebrews 10:19). Scripture also tells that He entered as a forerunner within the veil.

A couple of verses after Hebrews 9:12, the writer says: "… how much more will the blood of Christ, who through the eternal Spirit offered Himself without blemish to God, cleanse your conscience from dead works to serve the living God." Old Covenant sacrifices cleansed the body which had become unclean through defilement with the dead. To know that cleansing brought the cleansed one great pleasure and satisfaction. He would not for his uncleanness be cut off from his people and his God. Our cleansing is in the conscience which might well have been defiled by the dead works of this life. Such a conscience might well also, under the insistence of Satan, keep us from the service in the holies or elsewhere that God desires. The writer is not speaking about the sins forgiven through our salvation, but the conscience scarred by the things we did yesterday or even later. This again is a work of the blood of Christ which takes place long after our original meeting with the Saviour; in fact, it takes place over and over again.

God is so pure, so holy, that nothing - even the heaven and His servants the angels - are pure in His sight. Also by reason of our association with the heavens, even these have become unclean. Through the blood of Christ these are now purified so that a holy people might through the Spirit enter therein week by week to offer thanks and praise. So, Hebrews 9:23 says: "… it was necessary for the [earthly] copies of the things in the heavens to be cleansed with these [animal sacrifices], but the heavenly things themselves with better sacrifices than these." 'Better sacrifices' sounds like more than one, but Christ's one shedding of blood in all its aspects provided everything that was required for that cleansing. That is another thing concerning the death of Christ for which we must be abundantly thankful. In spite of my wayward thoughts, my aberrant actions, I have a clear conscience through the efficacy of Christ's shed blood.

The common Israelite could never have even approached the tabernacle in the wilderness and later in the land without a sacrifice in hand. Such audacity would have caused sudden death. Even those chosen as priests, and their helpers the sons of Levi, had no occasion to enter within the veil that separated their domain, the holy place, from God's holiest of all. Again, to change this was to invite death. The High Priest, once in the year with no one else around, had the obligation to make atonement in that location; such was life under the Old Covenant. But under the New Covenant we have a different situation altogether. Hebrews 10:19-22 states: "Therefore, brethren, since we have confidence to enter the holy place by the blood of Jesus, by a new and living way which He inaugurated for us … let us draw near."

Additional to the purchases by the blood, then, we have another attribute of the blood of Christ: the confidence to go where man never before was allowed to venture, the assurance that we as a holy priesthood are invited within a veil still in place in the heavenly sanctuary. In the Spirit we enter; by the Spirit we praise; through the Son our praise is accepted by the Father of the Lord Jesus who delights to hear His Son well-spoken of in our sacred breathings of prayer and song.

Hebrews 12:18-24 is an exciting passage of Scripture, describing as it does the parallel of what Israel was brought to at Mt. Sinai. But ours is heavenly and spiritual and concludes with our coming to Jesus the mediator of a new covenant, and to the sprinkled blood, which speaks better than the blood of Abel. The blood of Exodus 24:1-8 which ushered in the Old Covenant between God and Israel involved the blood of Burnt offerings and Peace offerings collected in basins and sprinkling the book of the covenant, the tabernacle and furniture and the people. All that was accomplished on the profession of the people to obedience: "All that the Lord has spoken we will do and be obedient." That was not their salvation; it was their collective pledge to obedient service to the God who had saved them. The blood of sprinkling here is the sweet savour blood of Christ mentioned here and in 1 Peter 1:2, not to do with our salvation, but to do with the effectiveness of Christ's blood to sprinkle God's new covenant people who will then by His grace serve our God and Master faithfully. This is yet another vital part of the work of the blood of the Saviour.

Verse 12 of the thirteenth chapter of Hebrews adds another facet of the work of His blood: "Therefore Jesus also, that He might sanctify the people through His own blood, suffered outside the gate." There are several aspects of sanctification, all effected by means of the shed blood of Christ. There is the once for all sanctification experienced by all who trust in Christ, accomplished at the point of salvation. Of this 2 Thessalonians 2:13 states: "… God has chosen you from the beginning for salvation through sanctification by the Spirit and faith in the truth." Hebrews 10:10 adds: "By this [God's] will we have been sanctified through the offering of the body of Jesus Christ once for all."

And Hebrews 10:14 follows that statement with solid proof of eternal salvation through faith in Christ with these words: "For by one offering He has perfected for all time those who are sanctified." There is, however, a second aspect of salvation that requires some reaction on the part of each of us. 1 John 3:3 says: "And everyone who has this hope [the hope of seeing Christ one day and being like Him] fixed on Him purifies himself, just as He is pure." Paul states to the Thessalonian Church this fact in two Scriptures: "For this is the will of God, your sanctification … that each of you know how to possess his own vessel [body] in sanctification and honor" (1 Thess.4:3-4). And in 1 Thessalonians 5:23: "Now may the God of peace Himself sanctify you entirely; and may your spirit and soul and body be preserved complete, without blame at the coming of our Lord Jesus Christ."

This type of sanctification is a daily washing of ourselves of our sins in the presence of God and an ongoing setting of ourselves apart as wholly for the Lord. The type of sanctification mentioned in Hebrews 13:12, however, is the sanctification of a people once for all, making them a "holy" nation. That, too, was accomplished through the blood shed at Calvary. It demands of that people that they suffer reproach with the One they serve while they wait for that heavenly city which is still to come.

We have, as believers, the Holy Spirit dwelling within, leading us into all the truth, directing us away from the defiling things of this world and pointing us in our thoughts to the Lord Jesus whom He magnifies. Between the Spirit and the blood we have little excuse not to be giving to God to the extent of our God-given ability.

In verse 20 of Hebrews 13 is mentioned the blood once again, this time in connection with resurrection: "Now the God of peace, who brought up from the dead the great Shepherd of the sheep through the blood of the eternal covenant, even Jesus our Lord, equip you in every good thing to do His will, working in us that which is pleasing in His sight, through Jesus Christ, to whom be the glory forever and ever. Amen." In our weekly Remembrance of Christ we proclaim the Lord's death, but we don't proclaim a dead Lord! Christ is risen from the dead, is alive and waiting till the Father says it is time to receive His

Church, and as Scripture says: "henceforth expecting UNTIL HIS ENEMIES BE MADE THE FOOTSTOOL OF HIS FEET.7"

"Christ lives in me," said Paul. Indeed, He seeks to live in each one of us, directing and blessing in new life - the life indeed - until at last we get to see Him face to face and see Him exalted to His rightful position, acknowledged by all as King of kings and Lord of lords. We enjoy all the blessings of new life and the promised resurrection through the blood of Christ. Jude had the right idea when he expressed in the closing doxology of his little letter: "Now to Him who is able to keep you from stumbling, and to make you stand in the presence of His glory blameless with great joy, to the only God our Savior, through Jesus Christ our Lord, be glory, majesty, dominion and authority, before all time and now and forever, Amen.8"

As God sanctified a people under the Old Covenant, the nation of Israel, so He has also sanctified a people under the New. This is evidenced by the sealing of the Holy Spirit, initially with those described in Acts 2:41-42: "So then, those who had received His word were baptized; and that day there were added about three thousand souls. They were continually devoting themselves to the apostles' teaching and to fellowship, to the breaking of bread and to prayer." Saved, baptized, added, continuing steadfastly in the apostles' teaching, fellowship, the breaking of the bread, the prayers - such we do according to His word to the glory of God and to the honour of His dear Son.

9: THE CUP OF THE NEW COVENANT IN MY BLOOD

While Old Testament studies might be interesting from a historical point of view, they would lose their sense of immediacy if it were not that they contained practical lessons for the people of God today. As Paul wrote to the Church of God in Rome: "For whatever was written in earlier times was written for our instruction, so that through perseverance and the encouragement of the Scriptures we might have hope.[1]" Peter tells us: "... for no prophecy was ever made by an act of human will, but men moved by the Holy Spirit spoke from God.[2]" Paul adds for the benefit of the Corinthian church and for ours: "Now these things happened to them as an example, and they were written for our instruction, upon whom the end of the ages have come.[3]" He also writes to his protégé Timothy, in his second letter: "All Scripture is inspired by God and profitable for teaching, for reproof, for correction, for training in righteousness; so that the man of God may be adequate, equipped for every good work.[4]"

These men had the Old Testament Scriptures. We are blessed to also have the further direction of the New. But there is much in the Old still to enlighten us. So God speaks to us today on many subjects, on many levels, but we must consider that He is addressing us concerning what He has revealed in His Old Testament word about the blood.

One of the final tasks of the Lord Jesus before He shed His blood was to institute His Remembrance. That consisted of the disciples doing just as He did on the night of His betrayal. He took a loaf and blessed. He blessed His Father, not the bread! Then He broke the bread and gave it to His disciples to eat. After this He took wine, gave thanks, and gave to His disciples, requesting that they all drink of it. He told the apostle Paul, furthermore, that in doing these things as often as they were commanded, His disciples would proclaim the Lord's death until He comes again[5]. That command has never been rescinded, so we do the same today. Luke, in his book of the Acts of the Apostles, indicates that disciples met for that service on the resurrection day, the first day of the week[6]. The book of Hebrews further reveals that in doing this we enter as a priesthood within the holiest of all in the Spirit, and continue not only in our Remembrance but also in praise to His God and Father through the Lord Jesus Christ.

Those who study the Scriptures (and that includes you, or you would never have read this far), may have appreciated that God uses several methods to emphasise His word to us. One of these is to repeat a pattern of teaching to us in concrete form through the Old Testament and also carry it forward into the New. For instance, the Holy Spirit often draws our attention to comparisons and contrasts and, so that we clue in to what is happening, repeats them: Cain and Abel, the one obedient to God and therefore God-pleasing and the other seemingly set in his ways, disobedient to God and not pleasing to Him; Judah, in Genesis 38 and his affair with what he considered to be a temple prostitute, really his daughter-in-law Tamar, contrasted with Joseph who in Genesis 39 rebuffs the wife of the captain of the guard and remains faithful to God even though it cost him years of freedom behind the bars of an Egyptian prison; Elijah and Elisha, contemporary prophets whose lives were so different, whose miracles were so different and whose interaction with people was so contrasting.

Then we go to the New Testament, where juxtaposition of men faces us with two thieves on the crosses beside the Lord - dramatic contrast. In addition to comparisons and contrasts pointed out to us by the closeness of people and events, we see God's principle of sin against Him over and over resulting in exile: exile from Eden for Adam and Eve; exile from the family in the case of Cain to a faraway place in the land of Nod, east of Eden; exile for Israel from their homeland of the northern kingdom to Assyria; exile for Judah, the southern kingdom, to Babylon; exile from the Great White Throne judgment to the eternal burnings inhabited by the devil, the man of sin and the false prophet.

Again, the Spirit repeats the principle of God setting aside the first so that He might establish the second. He began with Cain and Abel and continued with Esau and Jacob; He chose Joseph over his older brothers; He chose Ephraim over Manasseh; Gideon, the least in his father's house, was God's man rather than his older brothers; David was elected by God as monarch rather than his older male siblings; Solomon, the beloved of the Lord, ranked first over his older brothers. God today has chosen the spiritual over the natural as Hebrews 10:9 declares: "He takes away the first in order to establish the second" - this in relation to God's dealing with the covenants with His people. This leads us to consider several matters in a repeated pattern, a pattern which bears on the subject at hand, the blood - or rather, the cup of the New Covenant in His blood -   which is very much part of our activity on the first day of the week.

Leviticus 14 deals with the cleansing of the leper and the cleansing of the leprous house. In each case, two birds are taken and the one is slain over running water while the other has its tail dipped in the blood of the first so as not to deter its flight, and it is released to freedom - a clear picture of death and resurrection, both of which were necessary in the case of Christ for our salvation. If Christ be not raised, we are yet in our sins, of all men most pitiable (see 1 Cor.15:17-19). Leviticus 16 repeats the pattern this time with two goats, one to die for a sin offering and the other, the goat for azazel (or, as we know it, the scapegoat) to be confessed over and then led into the wilderness to be released free. This could be viewed, again, as a representation of death and resurrection.

Joshua 4 commands that two cairns be constructed out of uncut stones, the one at Gilgal from stones lifted from around the feet of the priests who bore the ark of the covenant into the raging waters of the Jordan in flood season, and the other built where the priests' feet stood which would be on the bank of the Jordan when the flood waters receded. The purpose of the cairns was to record permanently the wonders of the Lord fulfilled when the waters were backed up a long way in spite of the flood to allow the children of Israel to pass on dry land into their land of promise. But the two cairns were again a picture, the one in the Jordan of death and the other at Gilgal of new life where the reproach of Egypt was rolled away, a picture of resurrection. Micah, the prophet, states: "Remember ... from Shittim to Gilgal, so that you might know the righteous acts of the LORD.⁷"

It was between these two places, Shittim on the far side of the Jordan and Gilgal on the side of the Land of Promise, that Israel crossed the Jordan on dry land, among many other wonders. They knew God's blessing instead of Balak's curse. They followed under a new leader who would lead them into all the land. They knew the rolling away of the reproach of Egypt. God's righteous acts were manifested in continuing blessings upon His people. That remains unchanged under the New Covenant, for which we may be continually thankful.

Another comparison or contrast in some ways from the Old Testament is that of the two fellow prisoners of Joseph, prisoners who had upset the Pharaoh of the time and who had dreams from the Lord[8]. Troubled by their remembrance of the dreams, they each explained theirs to Joseph. The King's butler dreamed of a vine before him that had three branches bearing buds, then blossoms, then fruit. In his dream, the butler squeezed the fruit and poured it into Pharaoh's cup which he held in his hand. By God's help Joseph interpreted the dream: "the three branches are three days; within three more days Pharaoh will lift up your head and restore you to your office; and you will put Pharaoh's cup into his hand according to your former custom when you were his cupbearer. ⁹"

Pharaoh's chief baker who was the other prisoner, when he saw the favourable interpretation given to the cupbearer also told his dream. The results, however, were not as favourable and the cupbearer was told of his impending death. His dream of three baskets of white bread and sundry goodies resting on his head and being eaten by birds was interpreted by Joseph, again with God's revelation, that in three days he would also be released from prison but he would be hanged on a tree and fed on by carrion birds. Three days later, on Pharaoh's birthday, both dreams were fulfilled. The contrast shows a picture of life and death, but note - life and death in connection with wine and bread.

This is not the first mention of bread and wine in Scripture, for such was brought to Abraham by Melchizedek - an occasion connecting bread and wine to priestly service - but here the indication is that bread is associated with death and wine with life. Now, carry this thought over to the New Testament. On the night of His betrayal the Lord took bread and wine - separately, for they have not the same message. He commanded His disciples to do the same as they were called together, breaking the bread - a sign of the death of Christ - and drinking the wine, which He called the cup of the New Covenant in His blood. Hebrews 13:20 gives us a hint as to what to consider in taking that cup: "Now the God of peace, who brought up from the dead the great Shepherd of the sheep through the blood of the eternal covenant, even Jesus our Lord …"

Here, in the cup, we have our minds directed to resurrection and life. The symbols require a different treatment in thanksgiving. What is said for one is not that which pertains to the other. While certainly the wine speaks of His blood, it is not the oxygen-free blood of a dead Christ but a living life-giving blood applied that we might through it enter the holies with our praises. If we miss the difference, seeing only the blood of Christ's sufferings in the cup of wine, we miss a large part of our appreciation of the work of the blood and of the import of the New Covenant. This does not in any way demean the suffering of death for sin borne by the Saviour, but it should open new avenues of praise to us. If Christ be not raised we are yet in our sins, but by God's grace we stand as though sinless - pure in His sight in resurrection life, because of the blood shed at Calvary.

10: THE THREE CROSSES

Of the four Gospel writers who tell about the three crosses erected at the Place of the Skull that day when Christ's blood was spilled, only Luke tells us about the conversation between the two thieves. Matthew limits his comment to the observation that Christ was in the middle separating the other two, but they hurled upon Jesus the same insults that were emitted from the crowd. Mark says principally the same thing. John omits the insults of the two thieves. But Luke describes the conversation in detail, outlining the scorn of the one sufferer and the repentance of the other, followed by the Lord's calm promise to him that he would that day be with the Lord in Paradise[1].

Christ will always be the great divider, separating the lost from the redeemed. He had nothing to say to the one; nothing but promise to the other. The apostle Paul also spoke to the Corinthians: "For the word of the cross is foolishness to those who are perishing, but to us who are being saved it is the power of God.²'" Here again the centre cross and the One upon it is the great divider. Men must decide which side they are on - the foolishness side or the side of the power of God. The choice looms before men, but once made causes the believer to look back and see inscribed on that cross for us: chosen in Christ before the foundation of the world[3].

The crucifixion probably occurred not on that green hill far away, but on the flat Place of the Skull in front of the rock formation that resembles a human skull. Across the street from Calvary is a cave with a sign on it that identifies it as one of Solomon's mines; not a mine for metals but a mine for the golden stones cut out with great saws and shaped across the street at that ancient rock quarry at Calvary. From there the stones that were taken from that particular mine and shaped exactly fit the specifications for placement in the temple and required no sound of axe or hammer on site while the building was being erected[4]. It is just a thought, but in the case of living stones built up a spiritual house today we have each come from a different background and social structure, but the cutting and trimming to shape us for the Master's use had better be done at Calvary. If that scene doesn't shape me, grind off the bad spots, trim down the weak spots, then nothing else will. I need to return to that place where the blood was spilled often in my thoughts, prayers and thanksgivings.

Again to those three crosses: while physically three men hung each on his cross, the two for their own sins and the middle One for mine, spiritually there is another way of viewing Calvary - so done by Paul as he wrote to the Galatian churches.

Paul saw himself crucified there, as he says in Galatians 2: "I have been crucified with Christ; and it is no longer I who live, but Christ lives in me; and the life which I now live in the flesh I live by faith in the Son of God, who loved me and gave Himself up for me.[5]" He adds to that: "But may it never be that I would boast, except in the cross of our Lord Jesus Christ, through which the world has been crucified to me, and I to the world.[6]"

Get this picture in Paul's mind of three crosses - Christ in the midst, the world on one side and he (Paul) on the other. The two outer crosses separated by the one in the middle, but both on the outer crosses dying also - the world to Paul and Paul to the world. That is the way that it should be in my life also. Today, cameras and technical things like iPads and Smartphones also freeze time in pictures and such technology and video cameras are everywhere, as I say, freezing mini-seconds of time in photographic frames. Come with me for a moment of time to Calvary. The Gospel writers record the moment: Christ breathed His last, dead while the two on either side still squirmed and struggled with broken legs now, fighting to sustain life. Freeze that moment! For that is the weakness of the believing world of Christians today. I on the one cross, the world on the other, Christ crucified in the midst, but both the others struggling for life. I am not dead to the world. The world is not dead to me.

Is the purpose of Christ's death for the believer not fully realised as far as my Christian life is concerned? It would not be difficult to take me out of this world, but it is proving a far tougher prospect to take the world out of me. It all reminds me of Israel. It took one night to remove Israel from Egypt; it took generations to remove Egypt from Israel. Someone has said that we are all just one decision away from a whole different lifestyle. The decision may even have been made, but now needs to be worked into practice. Paul knew the dichotomy: "I am not practicing what I would like to do, but I am doing the very thing I hate … For the good that I want, I do not do, but I practice the very evil that I do not want … Wretched man that I am! Who will set me free from the body of this death? Thanks be to God through Jesus Christ our Lord![7]"

We need to cease the struggle and succumb to death to the world, for we cannot win in our own strength but in the strength that Paul found and is available to us in the Lordship and shed blood of Jesus Christ. Like the repentant thief, we have the promise of Christ for a far better future!

It was back in the American revival days of the late 1800's that men like Lewis E. Jones (1899), Robert Lowry (1876), and Elisha A. Hoffman (1878) wrote Gospel hymns that still resound in places where the glad tidings are sounded. The texts are written here to remind us all of the joy we had in proclaiming that Gospel sound: Lewis E. Jones of Yates City, Illinois wrote:

> Would you be free from your burden of sin?
> There's power in the blood, power in the blood.
> Would you o'er evil a victory win?
> There's wonderful power in the blood.

81 | BLOOD MOST PRECIOUS

There is power, power, wonder working power
In the blood, in the blood.
There is power, power, wonder working power
In the precious blood of the Lamb.

Would you be free from your passion and pride?
There's power in the blood, power in the blood.
Come now for cleansing to Calvary's tide.
There's wonderful power in the blood.

Would you be whiter, much whiter than snow?
There's power in the blood, power in the blood.
Sin stains are lost in its life-giving flow.
There's wonderful power in the blood.

Robert Lowry of Philadelphia, Pennsylvania wrote:

What can wash away my stain?
Nothing but the blood of Jesus!
What can make me whole again?
Nothing but the blood of Jesus!

Oh, precious is the flow,
That makes me white as snow!
No other fount I know,
Nothing but the blood of Jesus!

For my cleansing this I see—

> Nothing but the blood of Jesus!
> For my pardon this my plea—
> Nothing but the blood of Jesus!
>
> Nothing can for sin atone—
> Nothing but the blood of Jesus!
> Naught of good that I have done—
> Nothing but the blood of Jesus!
>
> This is all my hope and peace—
> Nothing but the blood of Jesus!
> This is all my righteousness—
> Nothing but the blood of Jesus!

Elisha A. Hoffman of Orwigsburg, Pennsylvania, among his 2,000 hymns - many of them very popular and sung widely today - wrote:

> Have you been to Jesus for the cleansing power?
> Are you washed in the blood of the Lamb?
> Are you daily trusting in His grace this hour?
> Are you washed in the blood of the Lamb?
>
> Are you washed in the blood,
> In the soul-cleansing blood of the Lamb?
> Are your garments spotless, are they white as snow,
> Are they washed in the blood of the Lamb?
>
> Are you walking daily by the Saviour's side?
> Are you washed in the blood of the Lamb?

> Do you rest each moment in the Crucified?
> Are you washed in the blood of the Lamb?
>
> Lay aside the garments that are stained by sin.
> Are you washed in the blood of the Lamb?
> There's a fountain flowing for the soul unclean.
> Are you washed in the blood of the Lamb?

These men were moved to write their hymns because of Revelation 7:14, which describes the innumerable band of martyrs that will give their lives during the Great Tribulation to come; for after the Lord comes back to the air for His own, a great leader/dictator named in Scripture as 'the Beast' will behead any who will not place his mark on their hands or foreheads, and will allow no trade to be undertaken with those who will not worship him. His end will come quickly and in the meantime myriads who will not accept his doctrines will perish, but they will have overcome him by the power of the blood of the Lamb.

How much better to accept that blood for the cleansing of our sin and sins today and to know rapture and blessing instead of the Tribulation turmoil - or worse, death - and its judgment consequences beforehand. There is no suggestion that we personally are to be washed in Christ's blood; it is the robes, the works, that are to be so cleansed. And our works, too - our habits, our daily comings and goings - require the work of Calvary to cleanse them and keep them clean. When we are often in confession we know more fully the power of the Spirit in walking with the Lord. The blood of Christ will never lose its power. When the aged John was ushered in a vision into heaven he saw a book with seven seals and eventually was given a vision of the One worthy to open the seals. He says: "And I saw ... a Lamb standing, as if slain ...[8]". The freshness of the death of Christ is ever before His Father and the host of heaven. As well as majestic and almighty, to all eternity He will be viewed as the freshly slain Lamb of God.

11: OUR GREAT HIGH PRIEST

It was not until His resurrection from the dead and His ascension to the Father's right hand[1] that the Lord Jesus Christ was named a priest forever after the order of Melchizedek, though the matter had been prophesied by David in Psalm 110:4: "The LORD has sworn and will not change His mind, You are a priest forever according to the order of Melchizedek." Melchizedek, King of Salem (which means King of peace), was but a type - a priest of God Most High, who blessed Abraham after his return from the battle of the kings. His name literally means "My King is Righteousness". It seems to me that he was not the Son of God in theophany or any such thing, but simply a man whose genealogy and death are not recorded, and so was made like the One whom he typified[2]. He brought out to Abraham bread and wine, refreshing him and his after the battle against the enemy kings and the vast journey to and fro that Abraham and company had had to endure. It is interesting to compare the picture of Christ doing the same for disciples weary with their journey.

But Christ's priesthood applies to more than the future, the 'forever' to which David refers; He is a priest today also. It is not our place to comment on how that affects those who as yet have not found their way into God's house, God's kingdom. "For what have I to do with judging outsiders? … But those who are outside, God judges.³" But the New Testament speaks mainly of the High Priest in His relationship not to individuals among the people but to the collective people as a whole. Hebrews 10:19ff deals with our entrance into the holiest on a Lord's Day, of which activity Scripture remarks: "not forsaking our own assembling together, as is the custom of some, but encouraging one another; and all the more as you see the day drawing near". Today as we look at the world in turmoil, we can hardly imagine the return of the Lord being far off. So we do encourage each other and endeavour to help each other along the way. We see the sights that cheer us on; soon we may hear the trumpet sound!

In Hebrews 4:14-16, Christ is seen in association with a people approaching the Throne of Grace in prayer: "Therefore, since we have a great high priest who has passed through the heavens, Jesus the Son of God, let us hold fast our confession. For we do not have a high priest who cannot sympathize with our weaknesses, but One who has been tempted in all things as we are, yet without sin. Therefore let us draw near with confidence to the throne of grace, so that we may receive mercy and find grace to help us in time of need." Possibly the writer has Zechariah 6 in mind where the High Priest is seen as the King/Priest with a crown of silver and gold upon his head and reigning and serving in connection with the temple, the house of God in its day. The Throne of Grace is a title used only here and is seen in connection with collective prayer with which the High Priest has some activity. This is one of the great differences between the prayer meetings of the Churches of God and simply praying at home. We would be poverty stricken if there were no private prayer in the home, and that is where children learn the immense value of waiting upon the Lord.

But we miss a tremendous opportunity of working in conjunction with our brothers and sisters and our High Priest if we "forsake the assembling of ourselves together as the custom of some is." There is benefit in two or more agreeing on something for which to pray. Christ is the majestic King of kings and Lord of lords, the One who shall reign forever and ever and put all His enemies under His feet. And He remains the Priest upon His throne, the kingly line and the priestly line separate before but now seen united and eternal since His resurrection. It is because of this we have a hope, says Hebrews 6:19-20: "This hope we have as an anchor of the soul, a hope both sure and steadfast and one which enters within the veil, where Jesus entered as a forerunner for us, having become a high priest forever according to the order of Melchizedek."

We have the hope of salvation which we are to keep active. 1 Thessalonians 5:8-9 tells us that we are to put on as a helmet the hope of salvation, for God has destined us for obtaining salvation through our Lord Jesus Christ. We have a further hope, (as Peter tells us in 1 Peter 1:3-4): "Blessed be the God and Father of our Lord Jesus Christ, who according to His great mercy has caused us to be born again to a living hope through the resurrection of Jesus Christ from the dead, to obtain an inheritance which is imperishable and undefiled and will not fade away, reserved in heaven for you …"

We have the hope that John writes of in 1 John 3:3 - the hope of seeing Christ. But Hebrews speaks of yet another kind of hope, a hope of week by week entering through the veil in the Spirit through our Lord Jesus into the very presence of God; and it is that hope which should anchor our souls in a world so like the sea whose waters cover most of it, casting up mire and dirt and in its tempest giving us little peace and rest. As our hope is, so should be our practice!

12: HALLELUJAH FOR THE BLOOD!

We have two responsibilities in meeting together to remember the Lord on the first day of the week: Our remembering will engender thanksgiving, and so it should. Who could not be thankful for having been brought from the dust and dunghill to sit with princes and to inherit the throne of glory? But we also gather for praise. There is a difference between the two. Thanksgiving (Hebrew: yadah) means an acknowledgment and is the expression of appreciation for what Christ has done and what God the Father has accomplished through Him; Praise (Hebrew: halal), is a step deeper, and is an expression of appreciation for who and what God is and who and what Christ is. The word includes meanings of to rave, to celebrate. The Hebrew yadah comes from yad - a hand, and todah - thank you. It is a raising of the hand in thanks and appreciation. Praise - halal - may take us beyond the blood on the doorpost and lintel, but it takes a bit more work, a little deeper study. Psalm 100:4 teaches that we enter His gates with thanksgiving, but we move further through His courts with praise. Such is our journey in worship, Remembrance by Remembrance.

Ezekiel, the prophet of doom preceding the captivity of Judah, is known more for enigmatic and judgmental prophecies than words about praise, yet the Spirit does give us some insight into the matter in describing God's house towards the end of his prophecy. Ezekiel hears the following: "Son of man, see with your eyes, hear with your ears, and give attention to all that I am going to show you; for you have been brought here in order to show it to you. Declare to the house of Israel all you see.[1]" And if that were not enough, the Spirit repeats the admonition to Ezekiel: "Son of man, mark well, see with your eyes and hear with your ears all that I say to you concerning … all its laws; and mark well the entrance of the house with all the exits of the sanctuary.[2]"

And then in about a dozen different verses is described what Ezekiel is supposed to notice particularly: features covered with carved palm trees, palm tree ornaments and cherubim[3]. There were palm trees and cherubim on the entrance walls, palm tree ornaments on the pillars and gates, and palm trees carved around the windows and on the doors. To get the significance of palm trees we must look at the Feast of Tabernacles: "Now on the first day [of the feast] you shall take for yourselves … palm branches … and you shall rejoice![4]" Then in the New Testament we meet them again on the occasion of Christ's triumphal entry into Jerusalem on the colt, the foal of a donkey:

"... they took the branches of the palm trees and went out to meet Him, and began to shout, 'HOSANNAH! BLESSED IS HE WHO COMES IN THE NAME OF THE LORD, even the King of Israel.[5]'" Palms are associated with praise. So are the cherubim, who are also seen flying before the throne of God crying, "Holy, holy, holy is the LORD of Hosts.[6]" Further, Revelation 7:9-12 shows: "... a great multitude which no one could count ... clothed in white robes, and palm branches were in their hands; and they cry out with a loud voice, saying, 'Salvation to our God who sits on the throne, and to the Lamb.' And all the angels ... worshiped God, saying, 'Amen, blessing and glory and wisdom and thanksgiving and honor and power and might, be to our God forever and ever. Amen.'"

Here, the myriads of martyrs slain in the Tribulation are seen in praise with heavenly beings before the throne of God. Now get the whole picture that Ezekiel gives us. The palm tree was to adorn the house of God in so many ways, especially about the entrances and egresses of the temple. Praise to God is what should also adorn the house today. "Oh, that men would praise the LORD for His goodness, and for His wonderful works to the children of men.[7]" "Worship the LORD in the beauty of holiness.[8]" Read Psalm 150, then praise the LORD! He is worthy to be praised. We are to be "a people for His praise, His glory through eternal days" as the hymn writer says[9].

Also essential to our worship and praise is the singing of hymns able to be participated in by our sisters in the Lord, the work of gifted authors and musicians (many of them also women) who contribute immensely to our service. Isaac Watts, one of the men responsible, is reported to have complained to his father about the dreary hymn singing and Gregorian chants droned out in the church congregation he attended, to which his father replied that if he were not happy about it he should get busy and do something - write some hymns that suited him. Action is always better than complaining. This, of course, he did, giving us some of the richest joyful church music and words of praise that we enjoy today. One hymn which we sing is the following:

> Come, let us raise a joyful song of Christ upon the throne.
> And join with heaven's angelic throng to make His glories known.
> Hallelujah for the Lamb that was slain on Mount Calvary.
> Hallelujah! Amen.

> "Worthy the One who died," they cry, "to be exalted thus."
> "Worthy is He," our lips reply, "for He was slain for us."
> Hallelujah for the Lamb that was slain on Mount Calvary.
> Hallelujah! Amen.

> The highest honours to receive the Lord all worthy is,
> And blessings more than we can give shall be forever His.
> Hallelujah for the Lamb that was slain on Mount Calvary.
> Hallelujah! Amen.

> Let all that dwell above the sky, and air, and earth, and seas
> Conspire to raise His glories high, and speak His endless praise.
> Hallelujah for the Lamb that was slain on Mount Calvary.

> Hallelujah! Amen.
>
> Creation soon shall join in one to bless the sacred name
> Of Him who sits upon the throne, and to exalt the Lamb.
> Hallelujah for the Lamb that was slain on Mount Calvary.
> Hallelujah! Amen.[10]

The source, of course, is Revelation 5, the chapter dealing with the revelation that of all that live in heaven or earth or beneath the earth, the only One worthy to administer the judgments of God by opening the seals of His book of judgment is the Lord Jesus Himself: "Worthy are You to take the book and to break its seals; for You were slain, and purchased for God with Your blood men from every tribe and tongue and people and nation. You have made them to be a kingdom and priests to our God; and they will reign upon the earth.[11]"

It would be difficult for us to refrain from adding our fervent "Hallelujah, praise the Lord!" Paul reminded the Ephesian Church that "[God] predestined us to adoption as sons through Jesus Christ to Himself, according to the kind intention of His will, to the praise of the glory of His grace, which He freely bestowed on us in the Beloved. In Him we have redemption through His blood, the forgiveness of our trespasses, according to the riches of His grace …[12]" Again, the blood is mentioned as central to the fulfilling of the purposes of God.

Peter also emphasises the importance of the blood: "… you were not redeemed with perishable things like silver or gold from your futile way of life inherited from your forefathers, but with precious blood, as of a lamb unblemished and spotless, the blood of Christ.[13]" The Roman church was reminded that they had been justified by blood - saved by His death, and that being so we are now being saved by His life. Not only do we in the present know the power of the blood, but martyrs of the future are recorded as overcoming the Accuser of the brethren who accused them before God day and night, Satan himself - they "overcame him because of the blood of the Lamb.[14]"

They did not even fear death when faced with it because of blood's significance. When Jesus shouted out from the cross with His dying breath "tetelestai!", ("paid in full!"), the price for our redemption was fully accounted for, our eternal salvation sealed. John writes: "… Jesus Christ, the faithful witness, the firstborn from the dead, and the ruler of the kings of the earth. To Him who loves us and released us from our sins by His blood - and He has made us to be a kingdom, priests to His God and Father - to Him be the glory and the dominion forever and ever, Amen.[15]" We add our Amen; and we say our Hallelujahs. Hallelujah for the Lamb! Hallelujah for His death and resurrection! Hallelujah for His precious blood!

13: A SUMMARY OF KEY POINTS

The writer to the Hebrews outlines his argument and then says (Hebrews 8:1): "Now the main point in what has been said is this …" Not everyone has the time, patience or even interest to plough through all the matters raised here and, like the noble Bereans, to examine the Scriptures to verify that such things are so. Here, then, are some major points raised, in case you missed them.

(1) While the whole idea of animal sacrifice seems to the modern mind repugnant, God shows clearly in His Word that He cares for animal life. He just cares for man more, and His holiness demands blood for atonement.

(2) The plagues carried out against Pharaoh and against Egypt were also carried out against Egypt's gods and against Israel, in part anyway, and were typical of judgments to be carried out in

Tribulation days yet to come.

(3) As and when the purposes of God come to fruition, Satan's activities on earth and against and among believers increase.

(4) The value that God places on His saints and His people can be measured in the severity of judgments that will occur in the Tribulation because saints have been harmed.

(5) The teaching of the offerings instituted at Mount Sinai take us beyond and deeper than the illustration of salvation taught to us by the blood of the Passover.

(6) My inadequacies, my uncleanness and my sin can have a real stumbling effect upon others and I must be judged for that influence as well.

(7) Offerings for sin, guilt and trespass are different from offerings such as the burnt offering and peace offering, which are not for the forgiveness of sin but to express devotion and fellowship.

(8) Blood is holy and is not to be eaten in any form either under the Old Covenant or the New. Its importance might be measured in the precedence it must receive in handling by the priests, among other things.

(9) What is termed the blood of sprinkling in the New Testament was not for salvation from sin but for dedication and sanctification of a people for the Lord.

(10) The greater the knowledge of God's things, the greater the seriousness of the sin.

(11) The time spent by the priests on the sweet savour offerings, an indication of the importance that God gave them, might well be an indication of the importance that we should place on that aspect of the death of the Lord Jesus.

(12) A Church or even the whole nation can sin; therefore we should include that in our confession.

(13) There were and are degrees of sin; there was no sacrifice for intentional sin then - it resulted in death.

(14) There is a difference between Christ's death for sin and His death for sins.

(15) Scriptures in Acts and Hebrews point us beyond the doorposts and lintels of the Passover to an application of the blood for the purchase of a people, their sprinkling, daily cleansing and sanctification, as well as the cleansing of the heavens for their entrance, their consciences for service, and the many blessings that are associated with Christ's resurrection and our own.

(16) The teaching of the two emblems used in our Remembrance is different, the one relating to Christ's death and the other also to His resurrection.

(17) From a "Paul to the Galatians" point of view, we have a part in the crucifixion, sometimes not altogether satisfactory.

(18) The work of our great High Priest is for a collective people.

(19) Our great Priest has to do with the prayers of a people in the prayer meetings of the Churches.

(20) In our Remembrance of the Lord there is a difference between our thanksgivings and our praise.

If a chief point had to be chosen it would probably be number 11: We should be giving more attention to devotion than thanksgiving, based on the God-directed orders to the priests of old. It is in this area at least where we will see the greatest change in behaviour, the result of learning and teaching.

REFERENCES

CHAPTER 1: NON-SACRIFICIAL BLOOD
[1] Ps.36:6 [2] Ex.20:10 [3] Ps.148:10 [4] Ps.150:6 [5] Prov.12:10 [6] Jonah 4:11 [7] Matt.10:31 [8] Heb.9:22 [9] Lev.17:11 [10] Gen.37:34 [11] Amos 8:10 [12] Zech.12:10 [13] Gen.4:10 [14] Gen.9:5,6 [15] Ex.7:20 [16] Ezek.20:6-9 [17] Josh.24:4 [18] Rev.19:11-13 [19] Is.63:2-6 [20] Rev.14:20 [21] Rev.15:3, 4 [22] Deut.31:30 to 32:52; Heb.11:9 [23] Rev.16:1-6 [24] Rev.16:3 [25] Rev.16:5-7 [26] Is.28:21 [27] Heb.10:28-29 [28] 1 Pet.4:17 [29] From "My Redeemer, oh, what beauties in that lovely name appear" by T. Clark (Psalms, Hymns and Spiritual Songs, 302)

CHAPTER 2: NON-ALTAR SACRIFICES
[1] Num.19 [2] Deut.21 [3] Ezek.18:32 [4] Ps.116:15 [5] Amos 1-2 [6] Lev.11:4; Lev.20:26; 1 Pet.1:16 [7] Num.19 [8] Heb.9:13 [9] Lam.1:13 [10] Ps.69:6 [11] Ezek.9:4 [12] Ex.12:13

CHAPTER 3: THE SANCTITY OF THE BLOOD
[1] Acts 15:20 [2] Lev.6:27-28 [3] Num.1:51 [4] Heb.10:31 [5] 1 Cor.11:30 [6] Matt.26:27 [7] 1 Cor.15:33 [8] Jer.13:1-10 [9] Lev.17:11

CHAPTER 4: SPRINKLED BLOOD
[1] Hos.4:6 [2] 2 Tim.2:15 [3] Phil.1:9-10 [4] Rom.2:18 [5] Heb.9:21; Heb.12:24; 1 Pet.1:2 [6] Ex.12:38 [7] Jn.13:1-17 [8] Lev.16:19

CHAPTER 5: THE BLOOD OF THE SIN OFFERINGS

[1] Mal.1:8,14 [2] Dan.9:4-11 [3] Num.23, 24, 25 [4] Micah 6:5 [5] Heb.9:22

CHAPTER 6: THE BLOOD OF THE SWEET SAVOUR OFFERINGS

[1] Heb.11:19 [2] Jer.14:12 [3] Rom.14:8 [4] Lk.16:1-13 [5] Homer W. Grimes [6] J. Walker

CHAPTER 7: AN ALTAR DRENCHED WITH BLOOD

[1] Arthur T. Doodson, 1938 *Bible Studies* p. 151.

CHAPTER 8: THE EFFECTS OF BLOOD FOR THE BELIEVER TODAY

[1] Jn.4:24 [2] Lk.24:39 [3] John Miller, *Notes on the New Testament*, 1 Timothy 3:15 [4] 1 Pet.2:9-10 [5] Acts 2:41-42 [6] Heb.9:12 [7] Heb.10:13 [8] Jude 24-25

CHAPTER 9: THE CUP OF THE NEW COVENANT IN MY BLOOD

[1] Rom.15:4 [2] 2 Pet.1:21 [3] 1 Cor.10:11 [4] 2 Tim 3:16-17 [5] 1 Cor.11:23-26 [6] Acts 20:7 [7] Mic.6:5 [8] Gen.40:1ff [9] Gen.40:12-13

CHAPTER 10: THE THREE CROSSES

[1] Lk.23:39-43 [2] 1 Cor.1:18 [3] Eph.1:4 [4] 1 Kin.6:7 [5] Gal.2:20 [6] Gal.6:14 [7] Rom.7:15-25 [8] Rev.5:6

CHAPTER 11: OUR GREAT HIGH PRIEST

[1] Heb.8:4 [2] Gen.14:18 [3] 1 Cor.5:12-13

CHAPTER 12: HALLELUJAH FOR THE BLOOD

[1] Ezek.40:4-5 [2] Ezek.44:5 [3] Ezek.40,41 [4] Lev.23:40 [5] John 12:13 [6] Is.6:3 [7] Ps.107:8 (KJV) [8] Ps.96:9 [9] From "Come Let Us Sing The Matchless Worth" by Samuel Medley (Psalms, Hymns and Spiritual Songs, 78) [10] From "Come Let Us Raise A Joyful Song" by Isaac Watts (Psalms, Hymns and Spiritual Songs, 73) [11] Rev.5:9-10 [12] Eph.1:5-7 [13] 1 Pet.1:18-19 [14] Rev.12:11 [15] Rev.1:5-6

MORE TITLES FROM THE AUTHOR

EZEKIEL EXPLAINED: GETTING TO KNOW GOD
The Old Testament book of Ezekiel is quite possibly the most intimidating book of the Bible for Christian readers and it is largely unread and often misunderstood - this concise book has been written to help correct that! This is not a chapter-by-chapter analysis, nor a verse-by-verse exegesis, but a topic-by-topic examination. The topics include:

- 'Ezekiel's Life and Times', to give us a flavour for the book; '
- Visions of God', investigating what is revealed of deity;
- 'Imagery and Symbolism', looking at some of Ezekiel's methodology;
- 'Ezekiel's Visions', God's ways of communicating with him;
- 'Of Him Bare all the Prophets Witness', seeing Christ in Ezekiel;
- 'Judgement on Judah and Jerusalem', and lessons for our own well-being;
- 'Judgement on Neighbouring Nations' - how to treat those suffering God's judgements;

- 'The Restoration of Israel', a look at the future, glorious for Israel and for ourselves;
- 'A Word to Shepherds', current direction to those who assume leadership of God's people; and
- 'The LORD Is There', an examination of the entities that will make up the millennium in Israel.

The book concludes with some bonus chapters by a variety of different authors, all related to the book of Ezekiel.

CALLED AS WE ARE

This collection of writings encapsulates many of Edwin's varied contributions to NT magazine over the years and covers a wide range of topics for all Christians today – including holy living, giving, worship, prayer and witnessing, with a special focus on exploring God's purposes for individuals and disciples called together.

MORE TITLES FROM HAYES PRESS

If you enjoyed reading this book, you may be interested to know that Hayes Press has many more books for you to appreciate. Hayes Press has its own imprint, with a wide variety of authors past and present, available in paperback and digital format. All of our ever-increasing digital catalogue can be found by searching online for "Hayes Press" at major e-book retailers. Paperback and digital versions of a number of titles can also be purchased directly from Hayes Press at www.hayespress.org.

Our Search for Truth imprint with books by radio broadcaster and Bible teacher Brian Johnston (podcasts available for download or streaming at www.searchfortruth.podbean.com) provides excellent reading material in a down-to-earth and conversational style, covering a wide range of topics from Bible character studies, theme studies, book studies, apologetics, prophecy, Christian living and more. Simply search online for "Brian Johnston Search For Truth Series" at major e-book retailers. Paperbacks of a number of titles can also be purchased directly from Hayes Press.

ABOUT HAYES PRESS

Hayes Press (www.hayespress.org) is the publishing arm of the Churches of God (www.churchesofgod.info) and is a registered charity in the United Kingdom, with a primary mission to disseminate the Word of God, primarily through the written word. It is one of the largest distributors of gospel tracts and leaflets in the United Kingdom, with over 100 titles and hundreds of thousands of tracts dispatched annually.

Hayes Press also publishes:
- Plus Eagles Wings, a fun and educational Bible magazine for children
- Golden Bells, a popular daily Bible reading calendar in wall or desk formats
- A wide range of theological and devotional books in paperback and digital formats.

www.ingramcontent.com/pod-product-compliance
Lightning Source LLC
Chambersburg PA
CBHW071306040426
42444CB00009B/1897